WITH ONE SPIRIT

With One Spirit

The Roman Missal and Active Participation

Jozef Lamberts

LITURGICAL PRESS
Collegeville, Minnesota

www.litpress.org

1   2   3   4   5   6   7   8   9

Library of Congress Cataloging-in-Publication Data

Names: Lamberts, Jozef, author.
Title: With one spirit : the Roman missal and active participation / Jozef Lamberts.
Description: Collegeville, Minnesota : Liturgical Press, 2020. | Summary: "Commemorating the fiftieth anniversary of the promulgation of The Roman Missal (1970), With One Spirit investigates the history of this text and the principles that impacted its development. In particular, Lamberts examines whether and how The Roman Missal encourages the active participation of the faithful in the liturgy demanded by the Second Vatican Council"— Provided by publisher.
Identifiers: LCCN 2020019287 (print) | LCCN 2020019288 (ebook) | ISBN 9780814665565 (paperback) | ISBN 9780814665817 (epub) | ISBN 9780814665817 (mobi) | ISBN 9780814665817 (pdf)
Subjects: LCSH: Catholic Church. Missale Romanum (1970) | Catholic Church—Liturgy—Texts—History and criticism.
Classification: LCC BX2015.2 .L35 2020 (print) | LCC BX2015.2 (ebook) | DDC 264/.02309—dc23
LC record available at https://lccn.loc.gov/2020019287
LC ebook record available at https://lccn.loc.gov/2020019288

Contents

Introduction

The year 2020 marks the 50th anniversary of the publication of the revised Roman Missal, promulgated by the Second Vatican Council. In the light of this anniversary, *With One Spirit:* The Roman Missal *and Active Participation* examines the genesis and the history of this revised Missal. More than that, this book focuses on the active participation of the celebrating community—one of the main goals of the Constitution on the Sacred Liturgy (*Sacrosanctum Concilium*), the first conciliar document—to see what changes have come about as a result of the 1970 revision. This book raises the question: How has the revised Roman Missal impacted active participation in the liturgy?

The first part of *With One Spirit* describes the gradual realization of the Roman Missal and demonstrates how the conciliar desire for the active participation of the faithful in the eucharistic celebration was the guiding principle for this revision. The second part is a critical examination of the way in which active participation has been incorporated in the different parts of the renewed liturgy of the Eucharist. At the same time, based on the results of the liturgical studies, we try to clarify in a pastoral way the meaning of the individual rites and their mutual coherence. We also want to formulate some cautious suggestions for a possible later revision of the Missal.

Our basic concern is to contribute to a more intensive experience and active participation everywhere Christians gather in praise and thanksgiving. They do this in response to the word of the Lord: "Do this in remembrance of me" (1 Cor 11:24-25).

Part One

Active Participation

*A Principle of
the Revised Roman Missal*

Chapter One

Active Participation as a Principle of Vatican II

One of the basic principles of the new Roman Missal that Pope Paul VI promulgated in 1970 is undeniably the active participation of the faithful in the eucharistic celebration. By emphasizing active participation in the liturgy, the Second Vatican Council (1962–1965) sought to end liturgical practice that, since the late Middle Ages, had become too clerical. Vatican II opted for a liturgy that, by the active participation of all the faithful, would become the true worship of the assembled people of God. The fact that the Constitution on the Sacred Liturgy mentions active participation at least twenty-five times proves its concern on that matter.

The Constitution points out that the liturgy presupposes active participation by the faithful based on their baptism. It points to the conditions and formulates a number of principles for ways to restore this baptismal responsibility.

Foundation of Active Participation

The Nature of the Liturgy

Articles 5–13 of the Constitution on the Sacred Liturgy present the theological basis of the entire Constitution by deducing the importance of the liturgy in the church's life from the nature of the liturgy itself. Liturgy results from Christ's work of salvation that continues in and through the church, which is the community of salvation.

As mediator between God and humanity, Christ is the instrument of our salvation and gives the fullness of worship to the Father, especially through the paschal mystery. This work continues in the church and culminates in the liturgy. So that the church may accomplish her work, Christ is always present in the church, especially in her liturgical celebrations. He is present in the eucharistic celebration in the person of his minister and especially under the eucharistic species, as well as in the other sacraments by his power and in the reading of the Holy Scriptures by his word. He is present when the church prays and sings. Therefore, we may consider the liturgy

> as an exercise of the priestly office of Jesus Christ. In the liturgy the sanctification of women and men is given expression in symbols perceptible by the senses and is carried out in ways appropriate to each of them. In it, complete and definitive public worship is performed by the mystical body of Jesus Christ, that is, by the Head and his members. (SC 7)

The liturgy is the summit toward which the activity of the church is directed. At the same time, it is the font from which all her power flows. Central to the liturgy is the celebration of Christ's paschal mystery as the perfect glorification of the Father and sanctification of men and women. The Mystical Body of Christ, head and members, fulfills this priestly action. The people assembled in the Spirit, united with Christ, their head, is here the subject of liturgical action. It is important to note that no distinction is made between the priest and the faithful, only between Christ, the high priest, and the entire celebrating community.

Liturgy Presupposes Active Participation

The entire celebrating community as the subject of the liturgy presupposes the active involvement and participation of all who belong to this community. That is why article 11 of the Constitution, where we find the idea of active participation for the first time, says:

> But in order that the liturgy may be able to produce its full effects it is necessary that the faithful come to it with proper dispositions, that their minds be attuned to their voices, and that they cooperate with heavenly grace lest they receive it in vain (see 2 Cor 6:1). Pastors of souls must, therefore, realize that, when the liturgy is celebrated, their obligation goes further than simply ensuring that the laws governing valid and lawful celebration are observed. They must also ensure that the faithful take part fully aware of what they are doing, actively engaged in the rite and enriched by it.

With these words, we become aware of the conciliar fathers' conviction that liturgy is not only, as the etymology of the word seems to presuppose, a work "for" the people, but also a work "of" the people. Liturgy is not only the realization of the work of salvation by the priest, in the name of Christ and the church, *for* the faithful but also a work *of* the faithful themselves.

Article 11 reacts against a mere ceremonial understanding of the liturgy. The Constitution does not deny the importance of the liturgical norms, but underscores that the "pastors of souls" must see it as their duty to bring the faithful to conscious and active participation in the liturgy. Prior to Vatican II, the strict observance of the rubrics was seen as the condition to make the performed actions into liturgy. Today, the active participation of the faithful is considered necessary for true liturgy.

Active Participation by Virtue of Baptism

Article 14 bases this participation on baptism as the incorporation in the people of God:

> It is very much the wish of the church that all the faithful should be led to take that full, conscious, and active part in liturgical celebrations which is demanded by the very nature of the liturgy, and to which the Christian people, "a chosen race, a royal priesthood, a holy nation, a redeemed people" (1 Pet. 2:9, 4-5), have a right and to which they are bound by reason of their Baptism.

The faithful have the right and duty of active participation because of their baptism, and not because of canon law or ecclesial authorization. The Constitution declares in article 29 that "Servers, readers, commentators, and members of the choir also exercise a genuine liturgical function," while article 28 says: "All taking part in liturgical celebrations, whether ministers or members of the congregation, should do all that pertains to them, and no more, taking into account the rite and liturgical norms." In other words, the nature of the liturgy presupposes the active participation of all the faithful because of their baptism while the liturgical norms indicate particular tasks for the meaningful performance of the liturgical celebration.

We can discern different degrees and functions in participation by the faithful at liturgy. I can be involved in my capacity as baptized person or on the basis of my ordination as bishop, priest, or deacon. I can fulfill a specific function as acolyte, reader, or a member of the choir; as one of the assembled faithful, I can participate very actively, or I can make myself a silent spectator.

Article 14 quotes Scripture when it calls the Christian people "a royal priesthood." Article 10 of the Dogmatic Constitution on the Church (*Lumen Gentium*) also speaks about the "common priesthood of the faithful." Further, it says that although this "common priesthood" and the "ministerial or hierarchical priesthood" differ from one another not only in essence but also in degree, they nonetheless are interrelated. Both originate from and participate in the unique priesthood of Christ.

The baptismal priesthood belongs to the "priestly people" as such, while the ministerial priesthood is realized in a personal charism instituted by the church. The ministerial priesthood presupposes the common priesthood and has the mission and role to lead the baptized in their communication with Christ. The church, the people of God, constituted by faith and baptism (confirmation), participates as a whole in the unique priesthood of Christ. In this way, it is the "integral subject of the liturgical action."[1] A division of this community into two explicitly separate classes, clergy and laypeople, liturgical actors and spectators, is completely wrong.

Conditions to Realize Active Participation

The Liturgical Instruction of the Clergy

The Constitution underscores that the intended full, conscious, and active participation of the faithful can only be achieved through the liturgical instruction of the clergy. Only when priests become imbued with the spirit and power of the liturgy will they be able to bring the faithful to active participation in an enthusiastic way. To achieve this the study of sacred liturgy must be included among the compulsory and major courses in "seminaries and religious houses of

---

1. Yves Congar, "L'Ecclesia ou communauté chrétienne, sujet intégral de l'action liturgique," *La liturgie après Vatican II. Bilan, études, prospective*, Unam Sanctam 66 (Paris, 1967) 241–282.

studies" (SC 16),[2] and the theological, historical, spiritual, pastoral, and juridical aspects of liturgy should be part of this instruction. And while liturgical instruction is more than giving classes in seminaries, such instruction will help future priests acquire the background and liturgical spirit to invite active participation by the assembled faithful in liturgical celebrations.

The Liturgical Instruction of the Faithful

The Constitution sees the liturgical instruction of the faithful as one of the chief duties of "pastors of souls . . . taking into account their age, condition, way of life and standard of religious culture" (SC 19). As an example, we can note the importance of liturgical catechesis in the preparation for First Communion and confirmation. We should not reduce this preparation to teaching responses to different parts of the sacramental liturgy and learning a few songs in order to prepare a beautiful event. Preparation for these sacraments is an opportunity to introduce the children into the spirit of the liturgy and help them become conscious of their role in the celebration of the sacraments, and further, in Christian worship. This liturgical instruction must continue on throughout the life of Christians. We can compare this to the *mystagogia* stage of catechesis in the first centuries of the church.

The Reform of the Liturgy

The Constitution speaks about a general reform of the liturgy itself in order to realize active participation. Several considerations determine this reformation.

Pastoral Objective of the Reform

A desire to renew the liturgy from a pastoral objective was an important component in the advice and suggestions that bishops, superiors of religious orders, and heads of universities submitted to

---

2. Today, this directive of the Constitution is not always evident in the theological faculties of a number of Catholic universities. On the contrary, they sometimes treat liturgy as an outside phenomenon.

Rome in preparation for the Second Vatican Council.[3] The Constitution solidified this desire when it states, in article 21, the "wish of the church to undertake a careful general reform of the liturgy in order that the Christian people may be more certain to derive an abundance of graces from it." It clearly determinates that both texts and rites should be written so that they express more clearly "the holy things which they signify" (SC 21). The faithful, so far as possible, should be enabled to understand the liturgy with ease and to take part in it fully, actively, and as befits a community. In the face of such a grand pastoral objective, the negative remarks expressed in the council chamber indicating that liturgical reform was merely a desire for novelty or archaeological hobby, had to be silenced.[4]

When certain signs, rites, or texts obscure rather than illuminate what they want to express, we have to look for new signs or restore those signs to their expressive originality. The scientific studies on the history of liturgy that were published in the last decades before Vatican II had contributed much to a better understanding of liturgical reform. At the same time, we are now open to new signs and rites that can evoke the same depth of understanding for present-day men and women, better than some signs that stem from another era and culture. The great international Catholic congresses of the 1950s contributed a lot to the beginnings of this reform, along with the input of so-called younger churches.

Tension Between Tradition and Renewal

We may not reduce such reformation to a few details. On the contrary, it has to be broad in scope. This does not mean that we have to transform everything or that we must have a *tabula rasa*. This would indeed be reform as an end in itself. A meaningful restoration or reform has to make a distinction between the essential and the nonessential, between content and form, between the unchangeable and the change-

---

3. See *Acta et Documenta Concilio Oecumenica Vaticano II apparando. Series Antepraeparatoria* (Vatican City, 1960).

4. Among others, Cardinal Alfredo Ottaviani used the expression *pruritus innovationum* in his intervention against the introduction of communion under both species. See *Acta Synodalia Sacrosancti Concilii Oecumenici Vaticani II* (Vatican City, 1970) Vol. I, pars. I, 18–20, p. 18.

able, the eternal and the temporary. Faithful to itself, the liturgy must express itself in signs, rites, and texts that touch, call, and encourage the men and women of today, that reveal to them the mystery of Christ and make them aware that they are the church. This renewal must incite them to the common worship of God and to engagement with humanity and the world. In this regard article 21 states:

> For the liturgy is made up of unchangeable elements divinely instituted, and of elements subject to change. These latter not only may be changed but ought to be changed with the passage of time, if they have suffered from the intrusion of anything out of harmony with the inner nature of the liturgy or have become less suitable.

Article 23 emphasizes that an accurate theological, historical, and pastoral investigation has to precede any reform. All three perspectives are important. The theological investigation discloses the deep content of one or another liturgical solemnity. The historical research demonstrates its origin and evolution. The pastoral reflection points to the necessity, meaningfulness, and possibility of a restoration, reform, or renewal.

The Nature of the Liturgy

The rediscovery of the nature of the liturgy as a celebration of the mysteries of faith by the assembled community of faith demands a renewed interpretation to better express what the Lord gives to his church. Article 26 formulates this principle:

> Liturgical services are not private functions but are celebrations of the church which is "the sacrament of unity," namely, the holy people united and organized under their bishops.
>
> Therefore, liturgical services have to do with the whole body, the church. They make it visible and have effects on it. But they also touch individual members of the church in different ways, depending on ranks, roles and levels of participation.

This important statement, which puts an end to an all-too-clerical liturgy, necessitates numerous changes in liturgical practice. Only then can the liturgy again become a celebration by the entire local congregation.

Article 26 is the first time that the Constitution speaks about the hierarchical structure of the church community. Even here, however, the congregation, the assembled people of God, stands in the very center: the people around the bishop. Each liturgical celebration has to be an epiphany of the church. At the same time, it must be church-forming.

The Catechetical Nature of the Liturgy

Article 33 opens a number of norms that justify the renewal of the liturgy from its catechetical and pastoral significance for the faithful. Liturgy is a means to glorify God by the sanctified community. Nevertheless, the liturgy is also an important instrument in the instruction of faith, especially in the Lectionary readings. When the assembled community of faith addresses its prayer to God, the liturgy is a true school of faith not only in the pronounced words but also in the signs and actions of the rite.

This catechetic meaning of liturgy received little attention in the last few centuries. In the years before the council, the instructive importance of the liturgy began to emerge; this became one of the most important reasons to urge the use of the vernacular.

The Culture and Traditions of the Peoples

The Constitution also motivates the renewal of the liturgy in order to obtain active participation that comes from the nature of the various peoples.

Accordingly, article 37 says:

> Even in the liturgy the church has no wish to impose a rigid uniformity in matters which do not affect the faith or the well-being of the entire community. Rather does it cultivate and foster the qualities and talents of the various races and nations. Anything in people's way of life which is not indissolubly bound up with superstition and error the church studies with sympathy, and, if possible, preserves intact. It sometimes even admits such things into the liturgy itself, provided they harmonize with its true and authentic spirit.

This article generally allows what Pope Pius XII (papacy 1939–1958) already partially allowed for specific regions by granting indults, or special dispensations. These indults stated that people in a particular region of the world could perform their own liturgy, their own expression of the universal prayer of the church.

Actually, this practice is a return to an age-old custom of the church. During the growth of the early church, different liturgical rites developed in the different regions of the Christian East, while the Roman rite continued to integrate elements from the Frankish, Celtic, and German cultures. Only when Christianity began to spread through the missionary activity, one neglected to adapt the liturgy to the culture of the new Christian communities. Nevertheless, very soon in the mission history one felt the need of such adaptation—evident in the Chinese and Indian rites controversy during the sixteenth and seventeenth centuries.

Renewal Decisions to Realize Active Participation

The Constitution not only indicates the conditions to realize active participation, but also formulates some concrete decisions about renewal of the liturgy.

The Use of the Vernacular

Perhaps the most remarkable change was permission to use the vernacular as the language of the liturgy. There had already been much discussion about this change in the years before the council considered it. A beginning was made with the partial introduction of the vernacular in the bilingual rituals. For many this was the most important condition to realizing active participation in the liturgy. They thought that the faithful would better understand the liturgy and feel involved once the vernacular replaced the unintelligible Latin. And while article 36 stipulated that the use of the Latin language is to be preserved in the Latin rites, the remainder of this article clearly opened the door for a wider use of the vernacular.

The regulation and approval of the translations belong to the local ecclesial authority in consultation with the bishops of the same language area, while the Holy See has to confirm them. Following Vatican II, a succession of ecclesial documents made the entire liturgy in the vernacular quickly available. It is important to note, however, that the use of the vernacular in our liturgy meant that a simple translation of the Latin texts would not suffice. What was needed was a usable English translation, which was then developed and owned by the International Commission on English in the Liturgy (ICEL).

The Simplification of the Liturgy

In view of active participation, the Constitution also opted for a simplification of the liturgy. Article 34 formulates as principle:

> The rites should radiate a noble simplicity. They should be short, clear, and free from useless repetitions. They should be within the people's powers of comprehension, and normally should not require much explanation.

More precisely in connection with the eucharistic celebration, it further defines in article 50:

> The rite of the Mass is to be revised in such a way that the intrinsic nature and purpose of its several parts, as well as the connection between them, may be more clearly shown, and that devout and active participation by the faithful may be more easily achieved.
>
> To this end, the rites are to be simplified, due care being taken to preserve their substance. Duplications made with the passage of time are to be omitted, as are less useful additions. Other parts which were lost through the vicissitudes of history are now to be restored according to the ancient tradition of the holy fathers, as may seem appropriate or necessary.

Later in this book, we will investigate to what extent this principle was taken into account in the new Missal. The Constitution itself gives three clear examples of rites that must be restored in the eucharistic celebration: the "common prayer" (SC 53), communion under both species (SC 55), and concelebration of Mass (SC 57).

The Promotion of the Communal Celebration

In its article 27 the Constitution asks to give preference to the communal celebration:

> It must be emphasized that rites which are meant to be celebrated in common, with the faithful present and actively participating, should as far as possible be celebrated in that way rather than by an individual and quasi-privately.

This applies with special force to the celebration of Mass (even though every Mass has of itself a public and social character) and to the administration of the sacraments.

Article 30 more concretely states that to promote active participation, the people should be encouraged to take part by means of "acclamations, responses, psalms, antiphons, hymns, as well as by actions, gestures, and bodily attitudes. And at the proper time, a reverent silence should be observed." Article 31 says that the rubrics of the revised liturgical books must carefully indicate the people's parts.

The new Roman Missal must be looked at in light of this principle. In connection with the eucharistic celebration, as mentioned numerous times already, the revision of the rites has to facilitate active participation of the faithful.

Richer Fare at the Table of God's Word

Partly under the influence of the biblical movement that demonstrated the great importance of God's word in church life, the Constitution opts for a greater place of Scripture in the renewal of the liturgy. Article 24 states it in this way:

> Sacred scripture is of the greatest importance in the celebration of the liturgy. For from it are drawn the lessons which are read and which are explained in the homily; from it too come the psalms which are sung. It is from scripture that the petitions, prayers, and hymns draw their inspiration and their force, and that actions and signs derive their meaning. Hence, in order to achieve the restoration, progress, and adaptation of the sacred liturgy it is essential to promote that warm and lively appreciation of sacred scripture to which the venerable tradition of eastern and western rites gives testimony.

From the catechetical nature of the liturgy, article 35 requires a broader, more varied, and adapted reading from Holy Scripture in the celebrations. Completely from a desire to involve the faithful in the liturgy, article 51 stipulates:

> The treasures of the bible are to be opened up more lavishly so that richer fare may be provided for the faithful at the table of God's

word. In this way the more significant part of the sacred scriptures will be read to the people over a fixed number of years.

In liturgical practice prior to Vatican II, the first part of the Mass—the Liturgy of the Word or the "Fore-Mass," as it was called—was not considered necessary for fulfilling one's Sunday obligation. Contrary to this, in article 56 the Constitution says that the two parts of the Mass, "the liturgy of the word and the eucharistic liturgy, are so closely connected with each other that they form but one single act of worship." It also says that the pastors have to teach the faithful to take part in the entire Mass. The faithful should be nourished at "the table of God's Word" (SC 51) as well as at "the table of the Lord's Body" (SC 48).

Return to the Sources of the Christian Liturgy

Article 50 states, "Other parts which were lost through the vicissitudes of history are to be restored according to the ancient tradition of the holy Fathers, as may seem appropriate or necessary." This expression derives from the Constitution *Quo primum tempore* by which Pope Pius V (papacy 1566–1572) promulgated the Tridentine Missal on September 14, 1570. At that time, a similar desire for change existed as a reaction against certain misconceptions about the liturgy practiced at that time. This prompted a move to review the eucharistic celebration from the oldest liturgical sources. Because of a lack of knowledge about these sources and because of the counter-reformation going on at this time, however, this plan could not be realized.

In our own time, thanks to critical research and archaeological discoveries, we have very old sources of both the Eastern and the Western liturgies. This return to the oldest sources is important to the discussion of active participation because it brings us closer to the grounding experience of what we aim for with our liturgy in that the liturgy from the oldest days of Christianity was essentially a common celebration.

Adaptation of the Liturgy

The oldest liturgical sources also demonstrate the existence of a pluriform liturgy, the possibility of adaptation and variety. In line with this, article 38 determines:

> Provided that the substantial unity of the Roman rite is preserved, provision shall be made, when revising the liturgical books, for legitimate variations and adaptations to different groups, regions and peoples, especially in mission countries. This should be borne in mind when drawing up the rites and rubrics.

Yet the possibility of adaptation seems not to be restricted to mission countries. In order to make active participation possible, Vatican II allows for adopting the celebration to the community while remaining loyal to the baselines of the liturgy. This is particularly important for eucharistic celebrations with children. Concrete possibilities can be found in the Directory for Masses with Children (*Directorium de missis cum pueris*) of November 1, 1973 and in the edition of the three Eucharistic Prayers for Masses with Children published in 1974.

Chapter Two

From Active Participation Toward an Ecclesial Liturgy

The strong emphasis on active participation of the faithful in the liturgy and the recognition of the eucharistic celebration as a community event raises the question: Is it better now to speak of an ecclesial liturgy?

From a Clerical to an Ecclesial Liturgy

Primacy of the Celebrating Community

The Constitution says that the liturgy itself presupposes active participation. It calls this participation, demanded by the very nature of the liturgy, a right and a duty because of baptism. It states that liturgical services are not private functions but celebrations of the whole body of the church. It underlines that every liturgical celebration is an action of Christ the priest and of his Body, which is the church.

In other words, the Constitution sees the liturgy as a community event in which the presider and the faithful each fulfill their own liturgical task that contributes to the whole. The *ecclesia*, the celebrating community of faith, is here made the subject of the liturgy. In this we are far away from the clerical liturgy as it developed since the end of the Middle Ages, and as it is expressed in the Tridentine Missal. This missal was entirely conceived from the perspective of the celebrating priest; there was no question of any input from the faithful. The eucharistic celebration emanating from the renewed liturgy is a grateful remembrance of Christ's paschal mystery by the sanctified faith community, gathered in the here and now.

Is the Concept of Active Participation Still Necessary?

We can therefore ask whether the term "active participation" is still adequate to use when we speak about the liturgy as a common celebration. Was this concept already burdened because of the situation in which it originated? Does this term not still isolate the celebrant and the faithful? Does it not presume that it is first the priest who makes the celebration and only then recognizes the right of the faithful to take part in it? Does the Constitution not say that the faithful have more rights than to join what the priest does? Is the liturgy not first and foremost the celebration of the faith community, of the local ecclesia, which by definition is a hierarchically structured community, one that has specific liturgical functions?

The notion of active participation may now be obsolete as it made the communal liturgy principally and practically possible. Yet we might ask whether the term should be retained when we see how the liturgies in our parishes are sometimes far from the ideal of a communal celebration. Will a liturgical movement always be necessary for the faithful to be aware of their part in the liturgy, so that it really becomes the celebration of the local ecclesia?

As early as 1976, Pierre-Marie Gy (1922–2004) stated that the expression "active participation of the people in the liturgy" does not do justice to the essence of what the people do in the liturgy.[1] Prior to that, in 1967, Yves Congar (1904–1995) designated the ecclesia or the local faith community as "sujet intégral de l'action liturgique."[2]

Toward an Ecclesial Liturgy

To fully do justice to the task of the whole faith community, with regard to the role of the presider and the faithful as well as of the liturgical ministers, we must speak about an "ecclesial liturgy." This expression points to the people of God who, called together by Christ, hierarchically structured, and animated by Christ's Spirit, celebrate their faith, in gratitude and praise, around the sacramental signs. In so doing, theology, Christology, and pneumatology are

---

1. Pierre-Marie Gy, "Liturgie," *Dictionnaire de Spiritualité*, part 9 (Paris, 1976) 911–912.

2. Yves Congar, *L'ecclesia ou communauté chrétienne, sujet intégral de l'action liturgique*, o.c., 241–282.

hereby honored. We see here church and sacrament interconnected. Insofar as we interpret ministry as a service to build up the people of God, a renewed theology of ministry can also be in line with this way of thinking.

Because we have underscored the role of the people of God who are called together, we can link the term "ecclesial liturgy" with the term "assembly." In the 1950s, the notions *assemblée* and *assemblée liturgique* received international resonance from France as an expression of the renewal in ecclesiology, sacramentology, and liturgical science. This was also influenced by the biblical-patristic *ressourcement* of the *nouvelle théologie*, in which the liturgy was seen as the celebration by the assembled people of God with the liturgical tasks of all participants.[3]

"Ecclesial liturgy" refers to the biblical *ecclesia*, derived from *ekkaleoo* to represent the Hebrew *qahal*, which means the congregated people. Thus, *qahal Yahweh* is called together to honor the presence of Yahweh. Transferring this concept to the new Israel, Origen could characterize this Christian people of God as "united by Christ's sacraments in covenant."[4]

Further Explanation of the Concept "Ecclesial Liturgy"

With the concept of ecclesial liturgy we see the liturgy celebrated by the church community as a realization of the people of God, the Mystical Body of Christ, and the temple of the Holy Spirit.

Sacramental Dimension

In the concept of ecclesial liturgy, the renewed ecclesiology and sacramentology find each other. In 1960, Karl Rahner (1904–1984) demonstrated that church and sacrament are inextricably linked together, constantly evoking one another.[5] His thesis was that we could only really find the essence of the church by immersing ourselves in

---

3. Aimé-Georges Martimort, "L'assemblée liturgique," *La Maison-Dieu* 20 (1949) 153–175. Id., "Précisions sur l'assemblée," *La Maison-Dieu* 60 (1959) 7–34.

4. Origen, "Homiliae in Numeros 16,9," *PG* 12, c. 701.

5. Karl Rahner, *Kirche und Sakramente* (Freiburg, 1960). English translation: *The Church and the Sacraments* (New York: Herder and Herder, 1963).

the sacraments. Our understanding of the sacraments also increases when we are more aware and better informed of what being church really means. After all, it is precisely in the sacraments that we fully express ourselves as church. We experience church intensely in the sacraments and are strengthened by this. The sacramental celebrations are privileged moments that make us aware, motivate us, and empower us to fulfill our mission as church in this world.

In liturgy the church experiences itself as the people of God convened by Christ to be obedient to the Word; to gratefully celebrate the coming of the Lord in his paschal mystery; to completely worship the Father; to be made one with Christ and with each other; and to be transformed and animated by the Spirit into the Body of Christ on earth. In the sense of meeting, ecclesia is the *activum* of the root word "people."[6]

The church is indeed the sacrament of the encounter with God, the earthly continuation of Christ, the primordial sacrament within sacramental salvation history, as Edward Schillebeeckx (1914–2009) stated in the 1950s.[7] The Constitution on the Sacred Liturgy twice denotes the church as sacrament, and this is also the case seven times in other Vatican II documents.[8]

When we see "sacrament" very broadly as salvation from God in physicality, the designation of Christ and with him his church, as in the patristic literature, sacrament acquires a rich meaning. God's salvation gained its full expression in the incarnation of his Word and continues to be realized in the church that is inspired by his Spirit, especially where it experiences its sacramentality in its liturgical celebrations.

Local Character

Since Vatican II, ecclesiology has strongly emphasized the local church as an epiphany, or realization, of the universal church. One

---

6. Joseph Ratzinger, *Demokratie in der Kirche* (Limburg a.d. L., 1970) 285.

7. Edward Schillebeeckx, *De Christusontmoeting als sacrament van de Godsontmoeting* (Antwerp, 1957). English translation: *Christ the Sacrament of the Encounter with God* (New York: Sheed and Ward, 1963).

8. *Sacrosanctum Concilium* 5 and 26; *Lumen Gentium* 1, 9, and 48; *Gaudium et Spes* 42 and 45; *Ad Gentes Divinitas* 1 and 5.

wants to see the church primarily as an event, a sacramentality that becomes reality here and now. One does not want to see the church as an abstract concept, but as a concrete reality: wherever the faithful come together hierarchically, united in Christ's name, the church manifests itself. The Dogmatic Constitution on the Church (*Lumen Gentium*), which indeed starts with the universal church as confessed in the Creed, declares that this church exists by and in the local churches (LG 26).

Here our full attention goes to the local churches, especially as they experience themselves in their liturgical celebrations around Christ's word and sacrament. After all, the liturgical celebrations are the special compaction moments of sacramental church-being. The church is entirely sacrament in its liturgy. This is what article 10 of the Constitution on the Sacred Liturgy says: "the liturgy is the summit toward which the activity of the Church is directed; it is also the source from which all its power flows."

Celebrating Community

Such emphasis on the local church as active subject of the liturgy and as manifestation and experience of being church, presupposes by definition the active involvement and commitment of all who make up this church community. Here every one of the faith community that has come together has his or her own task and responsibility so that the liturgy can really be what it essentially needs to be. By their active participation in the celebration through prayer, song, assent, attitude, and communion, the faithful make room for the experience and expression of faith by the community, for the realization of the encounter with God, and the sacramental presence of Christ's paschal mystery. Some have a more specific task as lector, cantor, minister, or celebrant. All these functions, however, are services within the celebrating community, functions that we can distinguish but not separate.

In the full sense of the word, the priest is not the only celebrant: the whole community celebrates. It has only been since the late Middle Ages, when the liturgy developed into a clerical liturgy, that one applied the term "celebrant" to the priest.[9] In ancient times,

---

9. B. Droste, *"Celebrare" in der Römischen Liturgiesprache. Eine liturgie-theologische Untersuchung* (Munich, 1963).

the priest in his liturgical function was called *proestoos*, literally, he who stands over.

Gathered in the Holy Spirit

With the expression "ecclesial liturgy" we also want to point out the role of the Holy Spirit in the liturgy. The ecclesia was born when the Holy Spirit descended upon the apostles (Acts 2). The glorified Christ continues to work in his church through his Spirit. This is confirmed in Scripture: "God has sent the Spirit of his Son into our hearts, crying: Abba, Father" (Gal 4:6, cf. Rom 8:15); "be filled with the Spirit, addressing one another [in] psalms and hymns and spiritual songs" (Eph 5:18-19); "No one can say 'Jesus is Lord' except by the holy Spirit" (1 Cor 12:3).

To the extent that the church lets itself be inspired and propelled by the Spirit it becomes the Body of Christ, that is, the sacrament of God's salvation. Not only church and sacrament belong together, but also church and Spirit. In fact, there is an inseparable bond between ecclesiology, sacramentology, and pneumatology. With Walter Kasper (b. 1933) we can call the church a "sacrament of the Spirit."[10]

When the church fully experiences itself in the liturgy and from there is sent to be the Body of Christ in this world, it must invoke the Spirit. Therefore, the renewed liturgy of the eucharistic celebration pays more attention to the epiclesis, that is, the invocation of the Holy Spirit during the eucharistic prayer.

Common Mission

An important consequence of this rediscovery of the working of the Spirit in the church is that each of the participants in the eucharistic celebration needs to be inspired by the Spirit. This is in order to give shape to the church as the Body of Christ in this world, the sacrament of salvation for humankind. This is each person's responsibility within his or her own concrete life situation. To celebrate the Eucharist is certainly not a noncommittal event: active participation in the celebration should lead to an active engagement in the world.

---

10. Walter Kasper, "*Die Kirche als Sakrament des Geistes*," ed. W. Kasper and G. Sauter, *Kirche Ort des Geistes* (Freiburg, 1976) 141.

Ministerial and Common Priesthood

Our approach to Christian worship as ecclesial liturgy does not detract from the distinction between common and ministerial priesthood. On the contrary, where we see the ecclesia as a hierarchically structured people of God, it evokes this distinction and, at the same time, the involvement of both.

We already pointed out that the ecclesia as a whole, by virtue of baptism and confirmation, participates in the unique priesthood of Christ: this is what we call the common priesthood. Within and not above this community we must distinguish certain ministries that build up and allow the community to function: that is the ministerial priesthood. Through the sacrament of Holy Orders the Spirit creates a special relationship within the community, which consists in serving the priesthood of the community. On the one hand, this ministry expresses in a special way the priestly mission of the whole church community: *repraesentatio ecclesiae*. On the other hand, by a special and personal charisma, the priest is ordained to the sacramental representation of Christ's power of attorney within the community: *repraesentatio Christi*.

According to the Decree on the Ministry and Life of Priests (*Presbyterorum Ordinis*) (2) the individual character of the ministerial priesthood seems to be that it represents Christ as head of the faith community: *in persona Christi Capitis*. This text immediately evokes the image of the church as Mystical Body of Christ. While Christ is the one head of the church, the priest represents in a sacramental way Christ as head, in the concrete experience of the local church as the Body of Christ. Thus, the celebrating community becomes the full manifestation of the church as the Body of Christ, head and members, as ecclesia or structured people of God. If we do not forget the inspiring and unifying role of the Spirit, we can see the description of the individual character of the ministerial priesthood as a sacramental acting *in persona Christi Capitis*. The Spirit animates the congregation by virtue of its baptism and confirmation. By a special charisma the Spirit allows the ministerial priest to represent Christ-Head in that congregation, so that the ecclesia is fully present to be the sacrament of Christ in the exercise of its common priesthood.

In line with what we have said up to now, we would primarily like to describe the individual character of the ordained ministry as an ecclesial ministry. By practicing that ministry within the faith community, it truly becomes ecclesia and can fulfill its priestly task, which is to offer full worship to the Father, together with Christ in the Spirit, through the celebration of its faith mysteries. This approach does not separate the priest from the community but rather brings him deeper into that community. It places him in the service of the community and makes his acting as a *ministerium* a service to the common priesthood of the people of God.

Chapter Three

The Genesis of the New Missal

The Work of the Consilium up to the Synod of Bishops in 1967

The Council for the Implementation of the Constitution on the Sacred Liturgy

By his *motu proprio Sacram Liturgiam* of January 25, 1964, Pope Paul VI announced the establishment of a constituent assembly to see that the prescriptions of the liturgical constitution were put into effect.[1] On January 13, 1964, the pope had already ordered Cardinals Giacomo Lercaro, Paolo Giobbe, and Arcadio Larraona Saralegui to organize this commission, of which Archbishop Annibale Bugnini became secretary. In a letter of February 29, 1964, the Secretariat of State set forth the tasks of the assembly that received its name *Consilium ad exsequendam Constitutionem de Sacra Liturgia*. Its task was fourfold: (1) to suggest experts charged with forming study groups for the revision of rites and liturgical books; (2) to coordinate the work of the study groups; (3) to prepare an instruction explaining the practical application of the *motu proprio Sacram Liturgiam* and outlining the competence of territorial ecclesiastical authorities, pending the reform of the rites and liturgical books; and (4) to respond to the proposals of the conferences of bishops and to questions that might arise involving the correct application of the Constitution.[2] On March 5, 1964, *Osservatore Romano* published the

---

1. *AAS* 56 (1964) 139–144. This text is called "*textus emendatus.*" The severely criticized "*textus originalis*" appeared in *Osservatore Romano* on January 29, 1964.

2. Letter "Mi onoro di communicare," in *Documents on the Liturgy, 1963–1979: Conciliar, Papal, and Curial Texts* (Collegeville, MN: Liturgical Press, 1982) 77 no. 613.

names of the forty-two members of the Council (further indicated as the Consilium).

The first plenary meeting of the Consilium was on March 11, 1964. A general work plan was drawn up, and forty-two study groups (*coetus*) were installed, each composed of five to seven consultors and presided over by a relator. These *coetus* were indicated by their number and name. Regarding the renewal of the Missal there were the following groups: *coetus* 10, the Ordinary of the Mass; 11, the Scripture readings in the Mass; 12, the general intercessions; 14, the songs in the Mass; 15, overall structure of the Mass; 16, concelebration and communion under both species; 17, special rites in the liturgical year; 18, commons to Breviary and Missal; 18b, prayers and prefaces; and 19, rubrics of the Breviary and Missal. A first exchange of views on the concelebration and communion under both species took place.

During the second plenary meeting on April 17–20, 1964, among others, a first design of the instruction to implement the council decrees, the rite for concelebration of the Mass, and communion under both species were approved. During the third plenary meeting on June 18–20, 1964, Abbot Primate Benno Gut, OSB and twenty monks, by way of experience, held a concelebration according to the proposed rite. The Consilium approved the instruction, the rite for concelebration, and for communion under both species. The Consilium also allowed seven abbeys to conduct both rites *ad experimentum.*

In order to maintain contact with the various members and consultors, a leaflet was published from March 1964 on under the title *Relationes.* To meet the greater demand for information, in April 1965 the leaflet began publication as a monthly periodical, *Notitiae.* It contained the official documents concerning the liturgical renewal, the decrees of the Consilium, the answers to the questions and requests of the local conferences of bishops, reports from the plenary meetings, the reports of the relators, and so on.

First Step towards the Renewal of the Liturgy of the Mass: Instruction Inter Oecumenici (1964)

The instruction *Inter Oecumenici* to implement the Constitution on the Sacred Liturgy appeared on September 26, 1964.

Emphasis on Active Participation

To achieve active participation the instruction once again points to the necessity of a close, living union between liturgy, catechesis, religious formation, and preaching (IO 7). Care is to be taken that the churches are suited to celebrating liturgical services authentically and that they ensure active participation by the faithful (IO 90). "The main altar should preferably be freestanding, to permit walking around it and celebration facing the people. Its location in the place of worship should be truly central so that the attention of the whole congregation naturally focuses there" (IO 91). "The chair for the celebrant and ministers should occupy a place that is clearly visible to all the faithful and that makes it plain that the celebrant presides over the whole community" (IO 92). "Special care should be taken that the place for the faithful will assure their proper participation in the sacred rites with both eyes and mind. . . . Care is also to be taken to enable the faithful not only to see the celebrant and other ministers but also to hear them easily, even by use of modern sound equipment" (IO 98).

Changes to the Order of Mass

Article 48 formulated that, until reform of the entire Order of Mass, numerous points were to be observed, among them:

"a. The celebrant is not to say privately those parts of the Proper sung or recited by the choir or the congregation."

"c. In the prayers at the foot of the altar at the beginning of Mass Psalm 42 is omitted." This was a first step towards restoring the function of the Introductory Rites. Since the "secret prayer" is to be sung or recited aloud, it was no longer seen as a private prayer of the priest.

"f. The doxology at the end of the Canon . . . is to be sung or recited aloud. Throughout the whole doxology the celebrant slightly elevates the chalice with the host, omitting the signs of the cross, and genuflects at the end after the Amen response by the people." This means a simplification and a recognition of active participation in the doxology.

"g. In recited Masses the congregation may recite the Lord's Prayer in the vernacular along with the celebrant. . . . "

"h. The embolism after the Lord's Prayer shall be sung or recited aloud."

"i. The formulary for distributing Holy Communion is to be, Corpus Christi. As he says these words, the celebrant holds the host slightly above the ciborium and shows it to the communicant, who responds: Amen, then receives communion from the celebrant, the sign of the cross with the host being omitted." Here too, the rite is greatly simplified and the Amen of the faithful shows particularly active participation.

"j. The last gospel is omitted; the Leonine Prayers are suppressed." Several of these changes were already formulated during the great international liturgical congresses of the 1950s.[3]

Liturgy of the Word

The instruction also spends a number of articles on the specific character of the Liturgy of the Word, such as, the epistle and gospel are to be read at the lectern facing the people, and that a lector reads the epistle while the celebrant sits and listens (IO 49–50). This puts an end to a one-sided clerical liturgy that required the celebrant to read each Scripture reading. It is a real recognition of the function of the lector within the liturgical celebration. Another important element of active participation is undoubtedly the introduction of the universal prayer at the conclusion of the Liturgy of the Word, which was not yet the custom.

The Use of the Vernacular

The instruction further stated that the territorial ecclesiastical authority may introduce the vernacular into:

> "a. the proclaiming of the lessons, epistle, and gospel; the univer-
> sal prayer or prayer of the faithful; b. as befits the circumstances
> of the place, the chants of the Ordinary of the Mass, namely, the
> *Kyrie, Gloria, Credo, Sanctus-Benedictus, Agnus Dei*, as well as the
> introit, offertory, and communion antiphons and the chants be-

---

3. Already in 1948, the periodical *Ephemerides Liturgicae* started an investigation into the desires and proposals related to the reform of the liturgy. The international liturgical congresses started in 1951 at Maria Laach (Germany).

tween the readings; c. acclamations, greeting, and dialogue formularies, the *Ecce Agnus Dei, Domine, non sum dignus, Corpus Christi*
at the communion of the faithful, and the Lord's Prayer with its
introduction and embolism" (IO 57). Additionally, "The Holy See
alone can grant permission for use of the vernacular in those parts
of the Mass that the celebrant sings or recites alone" (IO 58).[4]

The Introduction of Concelebration and Communion under Both Kinds

The first completely new rites were those of concelebration and
communion under both kinds. The decree of their publication dated
March 7, 1965; the rites were to go into effect on April 15, 1965.[5]

The possibility of communion under both kinds was consider-
ably extended compared to the list in article 55 of the Constitution
on the Sacred Liturgy, also in the following years. Four methods of
receiving the blood of Christ were given: drinking directly from the
chalice, intinction, use of a straw, and use of a spoon.

Congress on the Liturgy in the Vernacular

At the initiative of the Consilium, a conference on the liturgy in
the vernacular took place in Rome November 9–10, 1965. During
an audience granted to the participants, Pope Paul VI stated:

> The translations published here and there prior to the promulgation
> of the *Constitution on the Liturgy* had as their purpose to assist the
> faithful's understanding of the rite celebrated in Latin. They were
> aids to the people untrained in this ancient language. The translations
> now, however, have become part of the rites themselves. They have
> become the voice of the Church. No doubt the text in the vernacular
> that now has its place in the liturgy must be adapted to the concept
> of all, even little and uneducated. Nevertheless, as you know, it must
> always be worthy of the very high realities it expresses. It must there-
> fore be different from the common language used in the streets and

---

4. For example, on November 18, 1964 the Belgian episcopate obtained the
permission to say the orations in the vernacular.

5. "Decretum generale 'Ritus concelebrationis et communionis sub utraque
specie' promulgantur," *AAS* 57 (1965) 410–412. *Ritus servandus in concelebratione
Missis et ritus communionis sub utraque specie, editio typical* (Vatican City, 1965).

public squares so that it can touch the soul and ignite the love of God in the hearts.[6]

The lectures during this meeting very quickly demonstrated the problems that arose with the literal translation of the Latin texts. Some words, concepts, and expressions had a different meaning when translated, and did not respond to the experience of the contemporary faithful. The translations once again made it clear how strongly clerical the liturgy had become.

All Kinds of Difficulties

Several attempts at adapting the liturgy to the needs of the contemporary faithful arose in this period, especially in the Netherlands, with the goal of creating an appealing and livable liturgy. These were known as "liturgical experiments," yet they were often unauthorized. The word "experiment" as conceived by the Consilium meant a tryout of the renewed rite with authorization from the Apostolic See, during a fixed time and by certain groups who would then report on this.

The Consilium resisted the unauthorized searches for a renewed liturgy. In this context, Cardinal Lercaro wrote to the presidents of the national conferences of bishops:

> A general and thorough reform of the liturgy cannot happen in one day. It requires time, research, slow elaboration, criticism and control. It asks patience for all. I wish you would ask this of the clergy, so these personal, hasty and damaging initiatives that God does not bless and that consequently do not bear fruit will end. On the contrary, they cause disaster to the devotion of the faithful and the wholesome started renewal. They also bring disadvantage to our effort because they are generally random initiatives. They end up throwing an antipathetic light on the work that is done with thoughtfulness, sense of responsibility, prudence and true knowledge of the pastoral work.[7]

The impatience and experimentation continued, so that the Consilium reacted again in December 1966, especially against the

---

6. *Notitiae* 1 (1965) 377–381, 379.

7. G. Lercaro, "Epistola ad praeses coetum episcoporum," *Notitiae* 1 (1965) 257–264, 259.

widespread use of the vernacular and the new Canons of local congregations.[8]

Very soon, there was a trend in some countries toward the distribution of communion by placing the consecrated bread in the hand of the faithful. The bishops found it difficult to suppress this practice. After repeated appeals to Rome by bishops from the Netherlands, Belgium, France, and Germany, Pope Paul VI decided in 1968 to give permission for the practice to the episcopal conferences that asked for it, with the understanding that the conferences were to take the necessary precautions. Authorization was given to Germany on July 6, 1968 and to Belgium on July 11, 1968.

Another problem the Consilium was confronted with were the so-called family eucharistic meals, celebrations of the Eucharist in private homes, usually followed by dinner. In the Netherlands the so-called ecumenical agape celebrations were often confused with the eucharistic celebrations. In the same country, there were eucharistic celebrations with novel and improvised rites, spontaneous eucharistic prayers, and sometimes, new kinds of music and songs in the vernacular. These problems forced the secretary of the Consilium, Archbishop Annibale Bugnini, to visit the Netherlands three times to ascertain the situation and discuss it with the local episcopate.

While Bugnini was still in the Netherlands, a photo report in the French weekly *Paris Match* of December 17, 1966 caused a lot of commotion in the international press.[9] It shows, among other things, photos of a Mass with jazz, a concelebration in the catacombs of Rome, a Mass in a private house in Belgium, a Mass with indigenous dances in Cameroon, and a communion service in Brazil. On the front page we see a boy who takes a host with his hand. This photo is subtitled: "Cet enfant en Hollande se donne lui-même la communion." Shortly thereafter, on December 29, 1966, the Congregation of the Rites published its reaction of disapproval.[10]

On the other hand, the Consilium also had to deal with attempts to stop the renewal, especially the introduction of the vernacular.

8. X, "'Expériences' liturgiques," *Notitiae* 2 (1966) 345–346.

9. R. Serrou e.a., "La nouvelle Messe. Les enfants terribles de la foi," *Paris Match* 923 (1966) 67–82.

10. "Declaratio Sacrae Rituum Congregationis et Consilii ad exsequendam Constitutionem de sacra Liturgia," *Notitiae* 3 (1967) 37–38.

The so-called *Una Voce* movement wanted to keep Latin, Gregorian chant, classic polyphony, and the solemn liturgy as the norm for liturgy. In April 1967 Tito Casini interpreted this position in a pamphlet titled *La tunica stracciata*.[11] This booklet, with a preface by the curial Cardinal Antonio Bacci, who was known during Vatican II as a fervent opponent of the vernacular, was a downright attack on Cardinal Lercaro and the Consilium. During the eight plenary meetings of the Consilium (April 10–19, 1967) on April 19, 1967, Pope Paul VI openly rehabilitated Cardinal Lercaro. The pope expressed his appreciation for the work of the Consilium and regretted certain facts that made this work more difficult.[12]

The Entire Eucharistic Celebration in the Vernacular

Very soon after the promulgation of the instruction *Inter Oecumenici,* several episcopal conferences asked Rome to confirm their liturgical texts in the vernacular they had approved. In a short time, they had a single text for the Ordinary of the Mass. Even before the instruction, the United States bishops conference first published its Roman Missal (*Missale Romanum*). Despite its bilingual title, it did not contain the Latin text. Therefore, the bishops had to complete the book by including the new Ordinary of Mass, the *Ritus servandus*, the corrections, and of course, the complete Latin text. The next Missal to be confirmed was the Latin-French Missal.

Although the Consilium officially disapproved the experiments with new Canons from various countries, it could not remain insensitive to the need expressed by it. It became clear to everyone that the Canon in the vernacular would soon come. On the other hand, since the autumn of 1966, some new eucharistic prayers were being worked on within the Consilium.

A second instruction to facilitate the implementation of the Constitution appeared on May 4, 1967.[13] This document also strongly emphasized active participation of the faithful. In light of this, some

---

11. Tito Casini, *La tunica stracciata. Lettera di un cattolic sulla "Riforma liturgica." Con prefazione del cardinale Antonio Bacci* (Florence, 1967).

12. "Allocutio Summi Pontifis Pauli VI ad 'Consilium,'" *Notitiae* 3 (1967) 121–125, 123.

13. "Instructio altera ad exsecutionem Constitutionis de Sacra Liturgia recte ordinandam," *Notitiae* 3 (1967) 169–194.

simplifications were made to the Order of Mass, such as reducing the number of genuflections and altar kisses during the course of the Mass. In particular, however, it was determined that from June 29, 1967 onward, the Canon in the vernacular could be said aloud at Mass in presence of people.[14]

This authorization, however, caused the problem of which translation to use for the Mass. The French episcopate presented its French text in June 1967 to the Congregation for the Doctrine of the Faith. On July 15, 1967 someone told France that the submitted translations showed that the Latin text of the Canon needed a revision. There could not yet be an official translation of a text that still needed to be changed. On August 10, 1967, the secretary of the Consilium announced that permission was granted to use an existing translation of the Roman Canon approved by the episcopal conference.[15]

Not even four years after the promulgation of the Constitution that had opted for a wider use of the vernacular in the liturgy, the opportunity to celebrate the Eucharist in the language of the local community of the faithful was obtained.

The Synod of Bishops in 1967 and the Renewal of the Eucharistic Celebration

The Reform of the Mass on the Eve of the Synod of Bishops

The Missa Normativa

From the beginning of its activities, *coetus* 10 (*De ordine Missae*) worked for a eucharistic celebration that would be a true common celebration and no longer a clerical event in which the faithful had to be present only for the sake of duty. This was to be a common celebration in which the entire faith community was involved. A sung Mass celebrated by a priest with a lector, servers, a choir, and singing by the congregation would be the starting point for every form of eucharistic celebration. All other forms would be amplifications or further simplifications of this basic Mass, which would therefore be

14. Ibid., no. 10 and 28.

15. Annibale Bugnini, "Communicatio ad praesidis Conferentiarum episcopalium," *Notitiae* 3 (1967) 289–296.

called "normative." This was not to exclude the other forms, but to make the normative Mass the basis or guide for all other forms, from the Pontifical Mass to the Mass without the presence of people.[16]

New was the fact that one now chose a completely different starting point. In the previous period, at least in the theoretical approach to the Mass, one assumed the Pontifical Mass as model from which one derived the other forms. This was the rubrical way. Within the liturgical movement, however, the Mass took a different approach. In practice, one started from the read Mass in order to make this a community Mass by means of songs and common prayers. In the new approach, the normative Mass would have a supporting hinge function that held the different forms together and made them meaningful. More importantly, this meant doing justice to active participation of the faithful as a constituent element of the eucharistic celebration.

This normative Mass as presented to the Synod of Bishops looked schematically as follows:

Introductory rites

- Entrance of the priest, while the people and choir sing the entrance song (antiphon and psalm)

- Greeting of altar and congregation with an adapted formula

- Short act of penitence with the entire congregation

- *Kyrie*, which is dropped when the Gloria is sung

Liturgy of the Word

- First reading from the Old Testament

- Responsorial psalm

- Second reading from the writings of Paul and other apostles

- Alleluia with verses

- Gospel

- Homily

16. X, "De Missa 'normativa,'" *Notitiae* 3 (1967) 371–380, 371.

- Creed

- General intercessions

Liturgy of the Eucharist

- Placing the gifts on the altar with an adapted formula that does not anticipate the idea of sacrifice of the Canon, ending with the prayer over the gifts.

- Eucharistic prayer spoken aloud with acclamation by the people after the consecration.

- The communion rite begins with the Lord's Prayer and the embolism, immediately followed by the rite of peace and the fraction rite. Throughout the fraction rite, the Agnus Dei is sung. Then follows communion.

Concluding rite

- Greeting, blessing and dismissal.

The New Eucharistic Prayers

Early in 1966, two books by leading liturgists involved in the work of the Consilium brought the issue of eucharistic prayers to the international theological forum. In his book *Eucharistie: Théologie et spiritualité de la prière eucharistique*, Louis Bouyer pointed out that the ideal eucharistic prayer did not have a unique form in the tradition, but complementary forms that influenced each other.[17] He believed that before moving on to new eucharistic prayers that would be modern in their expression but traditional in terms of content and structure, it would be particularly instructive and constructive to familiarize the faithful with the other classic eucharistic prayers.[18]

Cipriano Vagaggini, OSB, in his book *Il Canone della Messa e la riforma liturgica*, pointed out some shortages of the Roman

---

17. Louis Bouyer, *Eucharistie: Théologie et spiritualité de la prière eucharistique* (Paris, 1966) 437.

18. Ibid., 439.

Canon.[19] He demonstrated these shortages both from the perspective of liturgical renewal and from a critical comparison with
the old anaphoras. He came to a threefold conclusion. First, the
Roman Canon should be retained, provided there are some minor
but necessary changes that would not harm its structure and physi-
ognomy. Then he would enrich the Roman liturgy with a second
Canon (project B) with a varying preface, which can be used *ad
libitum*, and which meets as much as possible the ideals of biblical,
traditional, liturgical, and pastoral feeling. Finally, he would compose a third Canon (project C) with a fixed preface that could be
used in Masses without a Canon of its own, and that would give a
panorama of salvation history. Thus, by its eastern inspiration, this
Canon also would have an ecumenical interest.[20]

This caused the Consilium to consider the possibility of several eucharistic prayers. The plan was presented to the pope, who accepted
it on June 20, 1966, and created a commission to compose or look
for three other eucharistic prayers next to the Roman Canon. The
commission started its work in the autumn of 1966 and presented
four eucharistic prayers during the eighth plenary meeting of the
Consilium on April 10–19, 1967. Two of the settings went back
to very old texts: an adaption of the anaphora of Hippolytus and a
Latin translation of the Alexandrian anaphora of Basil.

The working group that had prepared these prayers provided
the groundwork on which they were built. Thus, the *Sanctus* and a
consecratory epiclesis before the institution narrative were added to
the anaphora of Hippolytus. In addition to a eucharistic prayer that
follows the Roman-Latin tradition, one also wanted a prayer that
was more inspired by the Eastern tradition.

To this end, Dom Bernard Botte wrote a Latin translation of the
anaphora of Basil. Most consultors received it favorably; however,
fierce resistance came from Dom Cipriano Vagaggini. The reason
for this was the age-old dispute between the Latin and the Eastern
church about the moment of consecration. In the Latin church this

---

19. Cipriano Vagaggini, *Il Canone della Messa e la riforma liturgica: Problemi e
progetti*, Quaderni di Rivista liturgica 4 (Turin, 1966). English: *The Canon of the
Mass and Liturgical Reform*, trans. and ed. P. Coughlan (Staten Island, NY, 1967).
20. *Il Canone. . . .*, 97–98.

moment occurred when the priest pronounced the institution narrative as commanded by Christ. The Eastern church saw this happen when the priest invoked the Holy Spirit over the gifts. This epiclesis was said in the East after the institution narrative, while the Roman Canon, without explicit mention of the Spirit, placed it before the institution narrative.

If one accepted Basil's anaphora, it would be normal to leave the epiclesis in its place. Dom Vagaggini believed this would create confusion for the Latin Catholics. The consultors came to an alternative solution: they would present to the Consilium the authentic anaphora of Basil and a eucharistic prayer in the Eastern style based on project C of Dom Vagaggini. The Consilium decided on April 14, 1967, "for pastoral reasons," not to present Basil's anaphora to the Synod of Bishops.

The Synod of Bishops and the Renewed Liturgy of the Mass

In connection with the reform of the liturgy of the eucharistic celebration, the Synod received eight queries: four papal queries and four queries from the *Argumenta*.[21]

The Introduction of the New Eucharistic Prayers

At the vote concerning the introduction of the new eucharistic prayers on October 25, 1967, of the 183 fathers voting, the majority, 128 bishops, said yes (*placet*), 22 no (*non placet*), and 33 yes with qualifications (*placet iuxta modum*). A number of the qualifications asked that the introduction of the proposed anaphoras would not mean an end to the option for new eucharistic prayers, but that the conferences of bishops themselves would be allowed to compose new ones. Some asked about adapted eucharistic prayers for children and juveniles. Other *modi* insisted on caution. Several said that the Roman Canon should always have the first place of honor and be

---

21. Before the start of the Synod, the bishops had received a bundle with the issues to be dealt with, titled *Argumenta de quibus disceptabitur in primo generali coetu Synodi Episcoporum*. This contained five questions about the reform of the Mass. At the start of the Synod, four queries from the pope were added. The first was identical to the first question of the *Argumenta*. For the course of the Synod, see X., "De Liturgia in Primo Synodo Episcoporum," *Notitiae* 3 (1967) 353–370.

used on Sundays and the more solemn feasts. It is clear that such a proposal denies the intention of the new Canons. On Sunday, the faithful are gathered together to celebrate the Eucharist; precisely to give this celebrating community a recognizable alternative, one desires new eucharistic prayers. A more positive approach was the proposal to prepare the faithful through an appropriate catechesis of the new eucharistic prayers.

The Change of the Formula for the Consecration

The second and third pontifical query dealt with the change of the formula for the consecration. The query was whether the words *"quod pro vobis tradetur"* should be added to the formula for the consecration of the bread in the new eucharistic prayers. This must be seen from the perspective that the consecratory words as pronounced in the Roman Canon should be regarded as untouchable, so that when introducing the new eucharistic prayers this formula should also be adopted unchanged. On the other hand, there was a conviction that the proposed formula better expressed the sacrificial character of the consecration. That is why the pope presented the matter to the Synod. Only 12 fathers voted no, 110 yes, and 61 yes with qualifications. Most of the *modi* wanted the meaningful addition to be made in the Roman Canon as well. Some wanted to change the verb *"tradetur"* from future to present in accordance with the parallel passages of Scripture.

The third query was whether the words *"mysterium fidei"* should be removed from the formula for the consecration of the wine. In the years before this was presented to the Synod, there had been much discussion around these words, whose meaning is somewhat unclear, which have no scriptural basis, and which cannot be found in the other liturgies. This explains the large number of votes, 42, for *placet iuxta modum*. Further, 93 fathers voted *placet* and 48 *non placet*. Some also asked to omit the words in the Roman Canon. Others asked that the words *"mysterium fidei"* should not completely disappear from the liturgy but should be used as an acclamation by the faithful after the consecration. One *modus* asked also that the verb *"effundetur"* should be put in the present tense, *effunditur*, as in the parallel passages of Scripture.

The Apostles' Creed

The fourth papal query was whether authority should be given to the episcopal conferences to use the Apostles' Creed as well as the Nicene-Constantinopolitan Creed in the Mass. This was motivated by a question from parts of the world where the illiterate faithful must know everything by memory and where it is not possible to learn two creeds, one for catechesis and one for the liturgy. A great number of fathers agreed: 142 *placet*, 19 *placet iuxta modum*, and 22 *non placet*.

The Normative Mass

The first query from the scheme dealt with the structure of the normative Mass. Before the twentieth session on October 24, 1967, Archbishop Bugnini celebrated such a Mass in the presence of the fathers on the Synod. Each of them received a booklet with the songs and prayers and the text of the third eucharistic prayer. In fact, this was not a good thing for the normative Mass because, by definition, it presupposes a celebrating parish community, whereas here critical-minded observers were present.

Only 71 of the 180 fathers voted *placet*, 43 *non placet*, and no less than 62 *placet iuxta modum*, while there were also 4 abstentions. The vague formulation of the question and the ignorance of the proper scope of what one should understand by "normative Mass" was the reason many voted *placet iuxta modum*.

It is striking that many bishops had apparently not seen how the normative Mass could make the eucharistic celebration with active participation of the faithful the basis for every eucharistic celebration. Previously, despite all pastoral efforts to involve the faithful, Mass was a clerical affair, whether one started from the pontifical or from the read Mass.

The Common Penitential Act in the Eucharistic Celebration

The second question from the *Argumenta* dealt with the introduction of a penitential act that differs according to the liturgical season or to circumstances, and in which the entire congregation participates. This question had caused some difficulties within the Consilium. The issue had already been discussed in the liturgical congress in Maria Laach in 1951, and in Lugano in 1953 the introduction of a penitential act for the faithful during the eucharistic celebration was explicitly debated. Josef Andreas Jungmann (1889–1975) then argued that this would be based on saying the *Confiteor* together, purified from later additions such as the names of the saints. After praying together the priest would continue with the *Misereatur* and the *Indulgentiam* in the vernacular. Jungmann thought that this rite should be placed at the end of the Liturgy of the Word as a transition to the Liturgy of the Eucharist. Moreover, in the time of Hippolytus there was a similar rite in the form of a sign of peace.

Through his proposal, Jungmann formulated a meaningful alternative to a custom developed within the liturgical movement. A custom had arisen in the 1920s of saying the prayers at the foot of the altar alternately between priest and faithful. In fact, this practice contradicted the origins of these prayers that, after all, were not part of the common celebration. The need for active participation made it necessary to find a rite that really was a common event.

The discussion about this question came back in *coetus* 10. The first question was that of justification. Could one add an element that was unknown to the Roman Mass when one wants to simplify the liturgy? The French delegation was opposed to the introduction of a penitential rite. One said that there were penitential elements in the course of the Mass that could be pointed out in catechesis. Others were in favor of introducing a penitential act instead of the prayers at the foot of the altar, which almost everyone agreed should be abolished. For this they referred to Paul: "A person should examine himself, and so eat the bread and drink the cup" (1 Cor 11:28). Furthermore, they saw a great ecumenical value in this, because separated churches and ecclesial communities attach a great importance to it in the celebrations of the Lord's Supper. At the voting within the Consilium, 28 of the 36 members agreed to adopt the introduction of a penitential rite.

The question remained, however, about its place within the eucharistic celebration. After a lot of discussion, two options seemed viable: at the beginning of the Mass after the greeting, or at the offertory rite in connection with the rite of peace. For the members of *coetus* 10 the moment of the offertory seemed to be the most meaningful. The Consilium, however, opted for having the penitential rite at the beginning of Mass, after the greeting, because another placement for the rite of peace could be interpreted as a violation of the character of the Roman liturgy.

At the Synod of Bishops, the question of where the penitential act was placed within the liturgy was not discussed. The question at the Synod was, should all Masses have a penitential act that differs according to the liturgical season or to circumstances, and in which the entire congregation participates? The result of the voting on October 27, 1967, was: *placet* 108, *placet iuxta modum* 39, *non placet* 23, and abstentions 10.

The Readings during the Liturgy of the Word

The third question dealt with the experimental introduction of three readings in the Mass, so that after a period of experiment one could judge the suitability of this practice. This issue had also been raised for several years before Vatican II in various liturgical studies meetings. In that light, the Constitution on the Sacred Liturgy had stated that the treasures of the Bible be opened up more lavishly (SC 51).

Within *coetus* 11, *De lectionibus biblicis in Missa*, there was a lot of discussion about the choice of the readings, about the number of readings, and about the introduction of a three- or four-year cycle. The preliminary result of this discussion was the appearance in July 1967 of the *Ordo lectionum pro Dominicis, Feriis et Feriis Sanctorum*.[22] This provided for a three-year cycle with three readings on Sundays and solemnities according to this scheme: an Old Testament reading, a reading from Paul or the letters of the apostles, and the Gospel. The result of the voting was: 72 *placet*, 41 *placet iuxta modum*, 59 *non placet*, and 8 abstentions.

Songs at the Introit, the Offertory, and Communion

Lastly, the question was asked of whether it should be permitted to replace the antiphons at the introit, offertory, and communion with other songs if the episcopal conferences judge this as good, and using texts approved by them. One hundred twenty-six fathers said yes, 25 no, and 19 yes with qualifications. There were also 10 abstentions.

---

22. *Ordo lectionum pro Dominicis, Feriis et Feriis Sanctorum* (Manuscripto instar) (Vatican City, 1967).

The Further Work Before the Edition of the Missal

The Activities of the Consilium

Ninth and tenth plenary meeting

During the ninth general meeting (November 21–28, 1967), the *modi* of the Synod, among other issues, were discussed. During the tenth plenary meeting (April 23–30, 1968) they discussed the introduction of the penitential act and the sign of the cross, the formularies of the offertory, the place of the words "*mysterium fidei,*" and the structuring of the Mass after the Our Father, which included the fraction rites and the greeting of peace.

As far as the offertory rite was concerned, the idea had grown that this rite had to be reworked thoroughly so that its own character could be more clearly expressed. The formulation of the Roman Missal, especially in the vernacular, gave the faithful reason to misunderstand the actual sacrificial moment of the Mass. The working group initially thought about simply bringing up the gifts and omitting the offertory prayers. The Consilium opposed this because it might lead to the offertory being seen as a careless gesture. That is why they started looking for shorter formulas that would avoid any misunderstanding by the faithful. During this meeting, a start was made with the General Instruction of the Roman Missal (*Institutio Generalis Missalis Romani*).

Introduction of the New Eucharistic Prayers

On May 23, 1968, the Sacred Congregation of Rites issued a decree by which the three new eucharistic prayers and eight prefaces were released for use starting on August 15, 1968. The standards that regulated their use also appeared.[23] In these new eucharistic prayers the new consecratory formula over bread and wine, with the abolition of the words "*mysterium fidei,*" were introduced. After the consecration, an acclamation was provided with the three formulae that are currently in the Missal.

---

23. "Decretum 'Prece eucharistica,'" *Notitiae* 4 (1968) 156. "Normae pro adhibendis precibus eucharisticis," *Ib.* 157–159. The same number contained also the texts of the new prefaces and eucharistic prayers, in *Ib.* 160–179.

Eleventh General Meeting

Before proceeding with the final compilation of the new Missal, these last issues were discussed at the eleventh general meeting (October 8–17, 1968): the lyrics of the hymns, the orations, the prefaces, and the votive Masses.

The Release of the New Missal

The New Order of Mass (1969)

The apostolic constitution *Missale Romanum* of Pope Paul VI appeared on April 3, 1969. With this document, he promulgated the renewed Roman Missal, revised according to a decree of the Second Vatican Council.[24] The Sacred Congregation of Rites decreed in turn, on April 6, 1969, that the new Order of Mass was to be used beginning with the new liturgical year that started on November 30, 1969, the first Sunday of Advent.[25] The new Order of Mass itself appeared on May 9, 1969.[26] It was introduced by the General Instruction of the Roman Missal that, also on November 30, 1969, would replace the *Rubricae generalis*, the *Ritus servandus in celebratione et in concelebratione Missae*, and the *Defectibus in celebratione Missae occurentibus*, which could be found in the first part of the former Missal.

The New Calendar (1969)

In the meantime, the new calendar had been prepared and published. It was promulgated on February 14, 1969 by the Apostolic Constitution *Mysterii paschalis*.[27] In virtue of the decree of the Sacred Congregation of Rites promulgated on March 21, 1969, it would take effect from January 1, 1970 onward.[28] According to the

---

24. Paulus VI, "Missale Romanum. Constitutio Apostolica qua Missale Romanum ex decreto Concilii Oecumenici Vaticani II instauratum promulgatur," *Notitiae* 5 (1969) 142–146.

25. "Decretum 'Ordine Missae,'" *Notitiae* 5 (1969) 147–148.

26. *Ordo Missae. Editio typica* (Vatican City, 1969).

27. Paul VI, "Constitutio Apostolica 'Mysterii paschalis,'" *Notitiae* 5 (1969) 159–162.

28. "Decretum 'Anni liturgici,'" *Notitiae* 5 (1969) 163–164.

council's wish, the new calendar focused on the annual and weekly celebrations of the paschal mystery.

The New Ordo Lectionum Missae *(1969)*

The new *Ordo Lectionum Missae* was published on May 25, 1969 and was the foundation of the new lectionary that was developed in the following years.[29] The Lectionary for Sundays and feasts was developed according to three principles. First, there are three readings: an Old Testament reading, a reading from Paul or the letters of the apostles, and the Gospel. Second, there is a three-year cycle for the lectionary readings. Third, there are the principles of thematic harmonization or semi-continuous reading throughout the lectionary readings.

The New Roman Missal (1970)

On March 26, 1970, the complete Roman Missal (*Missale Romanum*) was published. In this way, according to the accompanying document, the mandate given by Vatican II to renew the liturgy had been accomplished.[30] The new Missal was published as standard (*editio typica*) for the whole church. As soon as the individual translations and adaptations to the different countries and language areas were approved and confirmed by the Congregation for Divine Worship,[31] they would also have the force of law. The English edition of the Roman Missal came out in 1974.

The new Missal contained again the General Instruction (*Institutio Generalis*), the Order of Mass (*Ordo Missae*), and the *Calendarium*. When we compare these texts with those published in 1969, however, there are some changes. Most striking is the addition of a preamble (*prooemium*) to the General Instruction. It seeks on the one hand to demonstrate the doctrinal continuity between the decrees of the Council of Trent and Vatican II. On the other hand, it points out the necessity of the reform. The preamble also brings

---

29. *Ordo lectionum Missae. Editio typica* (Vatican City, 1969).

30. *Missale Romanum ex sacrosancti oecumenici Concilii Vaticani II instauratum auctoritate Paulo PP VI promulgatum. Editio typica* (Vatican City, 1970).

31. The Congregation for the Divine Worship was from May 8, 1969 one of the two congregations that replaced the former Congregation of Rites.

out the ties with tradition amid a legitimate evolution of forms and the criteria applied in the compilation of the new Missal.

The publication of the Missal was apparently defended against conservative groups who were suspicious of it and did not hesitate to condemn this as unfaithfulness to tradition. The Congregation for Divine Worship had already issued a statement on November 18, 1969 about the nature and purpose of the General Instruction.[32] It was an answer to the critiques about the doctrine that the General Instruction would contain, namely, that it was not a doctrinal or dogmatic piece but a pastoral and ritual document. This statement also announced the changes and the extension with a preamble. During the thirteenth general meeting of the Consilium (April 9–10, 1970), the final text of the new Missal was prepared and the preamble, approved by the Congregation for the Doctrine of the Faith and by the pope, who had explicitly asked for that preamble, was added to the General Instruction.[33]

The influence of reactionary groups within the highest ecclesiastical circles is also noticeable when we compare the final Order of Mass with the normative Mass of 1967. These circles apparently made use of the result of the Synod of Bishops, where only 72 fathers had voted yes, while 62 fathers had voted yes with qualifications. The reactionary groups interpreted these last votes, which in fact agreed with the principle of the normative Mass, as a rejection of the renewed liturgy of the Mass and as a demand for a revision that more closely matched the old form. They also managed to put pressure on the pope who, on basis of the many *modi,* decided for a new revision of the Order of Mass. As a result, the work was delayed so that the renewal of the liturgy, which could have been a fact already in 1967–1968, was not enacted until 1969–1970. On the other hand, we must note that the year 1970 for the publication of the new Missal comes just four hundred years after 1570, the year in which Pope Pius V promulgated the Tridentine Missal.

Many of the imperfections and deviations from the principles established by the Constitution on the Sacred Liturgy are due to this policy, whereby one had to make compromises. The members of

32. "Declaratio," *Notitiae* 5 (1969) 417–418.

33. X., "XIII Sessio plenaria Commissionis specialis ad instaurationem liturgicam absolvendam," *Notitiae* 6 (1970) 222–231.

the working group regretted this state of affairs and did not hesitate to express their dissatisfaction. Nevertheless, the new Missal offers many opportunities for the realization of active participation of the faithful in the liturgy.

Afterwards, new editions of the General Instruction appeared. When the second edition of the Roman Missal appeared in 1975, some changes were made to the General Instruction. The intention was to bring the text into line with the renewed liturgical books and other documents that had appeared in the meantime,[34] such as the expansion of communion under both kinds and the abolition of the subdiaconate. On Maundy Thursday 2000, Pope John Paul II placed his signature under another typical edition of the General Instruction. The Holy See promulgated it in March 2002 with the third standard edition (*editio typica tertia*) of the Roman Missal.

On November 12, 2002, the Latin church members of the United States Conference of Catholic Bishops (USCCB) approved a translation prepared by ICEL. The Congregation for Divine Worship confirmed the translation on March 17, 2003. We will refer to this translation in this book.

This Missal added new Masses and prayers for various needs and new feasts, especially of recently canonized saints. It added more prefaces to the eucharistic prayers and adjusted some of the details of how the Triduum is observed. The structure of the revised instruction remained largely unchanged, however. The number of articles grew from 340 to 399, while a ninth chapter was added. In the light of the fourth instruction, *Varietates legitimate*,[35] on the Implementation of the Constitution on the Sacred Liturgy published in 1994, this chapter deals with the adaptations that are the competence of the bishops and the conferences of bishops.[36]

---

34. "Variationes in 'Institutionem generalem Missalis romani' inductee," *Notitiae* 9 (1973) 34–38; 11 (1975) 298–308.

35. "De liturgia romana et inculturatione. Instructio quarta 'ad executionem Constitutionis Concilii Vaticani secundi de Sacra Liturgia recte ordinandam' (ad Const. Art. 37–40)," *Notitiae* 30 (1994) 80–115.

36. In the previous edition, article 6 briefly states that the episcopal conferences, in virtue of the Constitution on the Sacred Liturgy articles 37–40, could make norms that take into account the customs and the nature of the peoples. This phrase is omitted in the new article 21.

A reprint with some additions, the so-called *Editio typica tertia emendate*, was issued in 2008 under Pope Benedict XVI.[37] On September 3, 2017, Pope Francis issued the document *Magnum principium*[38] on his own authority (*motu proprio*). It modified the Code of Canon Law to shift responsibility and authority for translations of liturgical texts into modern languages to national and regional episcopal conferences. It also restricted the role of the Congregation for Divine Worship. This went into effect on October 1, 2017.

Magnum principium can be seen as a reaction against the instruction *Liturgiam authenticam*, published on March 28, 2001. This instruction gave rise to much discussion, both in terms of the underlying vision of what translation actually is and in terms of its concrete application. Pope Francis clearly required a new start in the cooperation between the episcopal conferences and the Congregation on Divine Worship in the translation of liturgical texts. He also made it clear that fidelity in the translation process involved a threefold fidelity: first to the original text, then to the particular language into which it is translated, and finally to the comprehension of the text by the recipients.[39] Especially by pointing to this last element, the pope actually reverts to one of the foremost conditions that Vatican II had set for realizing active participation. We will soon see what the conferences of bishops, with the help of ICEL, will do with this papal directive.

The Apostolic See recognized the Roman Missal used in the United States today in 2010, and the mandatory implementation date was the First Sunday of Advent, November 27, 2011.

---

37. *Notitiae* 44 (2008) 367–387.

38. https://press.vatican.va/content/salastampa/en/bollettino/pubblico/2017/09/09/170909a.html

39. "Without doubt, attention must be paid to the benefit and good of the faithful, nor must the right and duty of Episcopal Conferences be forgotten who, together with Episcopal Conferences from regions sharing the same language and with the Apostolic See, must ensure and establish that, while the character of each language is safeguarded, the sense of the original text is fully and faithfully rendered and that even after adaptations the translated liturgical books always illuminate the unity of the Roman Rite."

Chapter Four

Active Participation as the Basic Principle of the Roman Missal

When we read the General Instruction of the current Missal, it is striking how active participation of the faithful is always referred to from different points of view, so that it is not exaggeration to say that active participation is the basic principle of the Missal. It states that the very nature of the eucharistic celebration presupposes the active participation of the assembled people of God. There is an explicit reference to everyone's task within the celebration. This active involvement of the community should be expressed in communal prayer, singing, gestures, attitudes, and silence. From this, we can see Mass with the participation of the faithful as the new model for eucharistic celebration. The church building should be arranged in service of active participation, and even the texts chosen for Mass can facilitate this purpose.

Active Participation from the Nature of the Eucharist

The first chapter (GIRM 16–26) of the General Instruction, which deals with the importance and dignity of the eucharistic celebration, speaks several times about the involvement of the faithful (emphasis added).

Article 16: "The celebration of Mass, as the action of Christ *and of the People of God* arrayed hierarchically . . . "

Article 17: "It is . . . of the greatest importance that the celebration of the Mass . . . be so ordered that the sacred ministers and *the faithful taking part in it . . .* "

Article 18: "This will fittingly come about if, with due regard for the nature and other circumstances of each liturgical assembly, the entire celebration is arranged in such a way that it leads to *a conscious, active, and full participation of the faithful*, namely in body and in mind, a participation fervent with faith, hope, and charity, of the sort which is desired by the church and which is required by the very nature of the celebration and to which the Christian people have a right and duty in virtue of their Baptism."

Article 20: "[T]he greatest care is to be taken that those forms and elements proposed by the Church are chosen and arranged, which . . . more effectively foster *active and full participation* and more aptly respond to the spiritual needs of the faithful."

Article 22: "The Bishop should therefore be determined that the . . . faithful grasp every more deeply the genuine significance of the rites and liturgical texts, and thereby be led to the active and fruitful celebration of the Eucharist."

Article 24: "These adaptations consist . . . of the chants, readings, prayers, explanatory interventions, and gestures capable of responding better to the needs, the preparation, and the culture of the participants . . . "

Each of these articles stress that the local and personal circumstances, and the nature of peoples and groups are constructive for the concrete shape of the Eucharist.

Our Duties Within the Eucharistic Celebration

While chapter two (GIRM 27–90) deals with the structure of the Mass, chapter three (GIRM 91–111) discusses the duties and ministries in the Mass. With three references to the Constitution on the Sacred Liturgy, article 91 of the General Instruction clearly says:

> The celebration of the Eucharist is the action of Christ and of the Church, namely, of the holy people united and ordered under the Bishop. It therefore pertains to the whole Body of the Church, manifests it, and has its effect upon it. Indeed, it also affects the individual members of the Church in a different way, according to their different orders, functions, and actual participation.[1] In this

1. SC 26.

way, the Christian people, "a chosen race, a royal Priesthood, a holy nation, a people for his own possession," expresses its cohesion and its hierarchical ordering.[2] All, therefore, whether ordained ministers or lay Christian faithful, in fulfilling their function or their duty, should carry out solely but totally that which pertains to them.[3]

This article expressly confirms the ecclesial aspect of every liturgical celebration in the sense that had been in place since Vatican II, whereby we see the church no longer as a clerical institution, but as the people of God.

Articles 92–94 deal with the duties of those in Holy Orders. Here too it is striking that one always speaks of the presence of the faithful as the normative way of celebrating the Eucharist. Articles 95–97 deal with the duties of the people of God. This text indicates five forms of active involvement of the entire celebrating community: the common listening to the message of salvation, the common offering of the sacrifice, the common partaking of communion, the common praying and singing, and the common gestures and postures. A number of articles further emphasize the importance of the last two elements.

The Importance of the Outward Forms of Active Participation

The General Instruction strongly emphasizes the importance of the outward forms of active participation, which express that the eucharistic celebration is a common event, in which all must be actively involved. A liturgy that wants to be a community event calls for the input of all through common praying and singing, responding to what has been heard, and common actions and body postures. It is precisely on this point that the new Missal is very different from that of Pius V, which actually had no input from the faithful.

Common Prayer

Article 34 of the General Instruction refers to the communal character that belongs to the essence of the eucharistic celebration. This is expressed by praying in dialogue between the priest and the

---

2. SC 14.
3. SC 28.

faithful, and the affirmative response by the community to what the priest as presider prays in the name of all. This is not, as the article says, a simply outward sign of communal celebration, but it realizes the bond between priest and people. In it, the church realizes itself in its hierarchical structure.

Article 35 firmly says:

> The acclamations and the responses of the faithful to the Priest's greetings and prayers constitute that level of active participation that is to be made by the assembled faithful in every form of the Mass, so that the action of the whole community may be clearly expressed and fostered.

Article 36 points to other parts of the Mass as very useful for expressing and fostering the faithful's active participation. These parts, which are assigned to the whole assembly, include the penitential act, the profession of faith, the prayer of the faithful (universal prayer), and the Lord's Prayer.

Common Singing

Articles 40–41 of the General Instruction attach great importance to singing, "with due consideration for the culture of peoples and the abilities of each liturgical assembly." While it is not always necessary to sing, preference should be given to the parts of the Mass that are most important to sing, especially those that should be sung by the priest, the deacon, or the lector, with the people responding, or by the priest and people together. Here too, active participation is the motivating principle. We have to choose music that fits with the ability of the congregation and allows it to be fully involved by its song, in concert with the priest. Above all, we must take care that music sung during the Mass not be an artistic performance by the choir.

The Common Movements and Postures

The General Instruction also sees the common movements and postures as an explicit experience of active participation. Article 42 calls a common posture, observed by all participants, "a sign of the unity of the members of the Christian community gathered for the

Sacred Liturgy" because it expresses and fosters the intention and spiritual attitude of the participants. Article 43 presents some general principles about standing, sitting, and kneeling. Taking into account the culture of the people and the character of each part of the Mass, the episcopal conferences are authorized to formulate guidelines that are more concrete in this regard.

Common Silence

The General Instruction provides express moments of common silence. These are moments when everyone in the community can reflect on the liturgical event and join with the assembled, in one's deepest personal core, with what is said, prayed, sung, and acted out.

The Mass with a Congregation as the Normal Form of the Eucharistic Celebration

Chapter four (GIRM 112–287) deals with the different forms of celebrating Mass. From the very beginning of this chapter, article 112 considers Mass with a congregation as the normal form of eucharistic celebration because such Mass expresses the ecclesial character of the eucharistic celebration. It is the gathering of the people of God, who together and under the direction of the bishop, constitute the local church community *in persona Christi*, gratefully celebrate the remembrance of the Lord, and bring perfect worship to the Father.

Article 112 does justice to all the achievements of the liturgical movement: the renewed ecclesiology (people of God, local church), the Eucharist as common celebration, and active participation (what is in fact understood by common celebration).

Placing this celebration, with presence and active participation of the people as the normal and most explicit manner of eucharistic celebration, is a revolution with respect to the Missal of Pius V. The Missal of 1570, commonly known as the Tridentine Missal, was based on the celebrating priest; the presence or absence of the people actually made no difference to the celebration. In the Roman Missal of Paul VI, published in 1970, active participation becomes an integral element of the eucharistic celebration.

The Arrangement of Churches with a View to Active Participation

The introductory article of chapter five affirms the importance of active participation. It clearly says, "[C]hurches or other places should be suitable for carrying out the sacred action and for ensuring the active participation of the faithful" (GIRM 288). Article 294 pays attention both to the common character of the eucharistic celebration and to the peculiarity of the different functions, with reference to the active role of the faithful.

In connection with the places of the faithful, article 311 also explicitly refers to the promotion of active participation:

> Places for the faithful should be arranged with appropriate care so that they are able to participate in the sacred celebrations, duly following them with their eyes and their attention. It is desirable that benches or seating usually should be provided for their use. However, the custom of reserving seats for private persons is to be reprobated. Moreover, benches or seating should be arranged, especially in newly built churches, that the faithful can easily take up the bodily postures required for the different parts of the celebration and can have easy access for the reception of Holy Communion.
>
> Care should be taken to ensure that the faithful be able not only to see the priest, the deacon, and the readers but also, with the aid of modern technical means, to hear them without difficulty.

Texts for the Mass with a View to Active Participation

In chapter seven, on the choice of the Mass and its parts, we find again a strong emphasis on active participation in the introductory article 352:

> The pastoral effectiveness of a celebration will be greatly increased if the texts of the readings, the prayers, and the liturgical chants correspond as aptly as possible to the needs, the preparation, and culture of the participants. This will be achieved by appropriate use of the many possibilities of choice described below.
>
> Hence in arranging the celebration of Mass, the priest should be attentive rather to the common spiritual good of the people of God than to his own inclinations. He should also remember that choices

of this kind are to be made in harmony with those who exercise some part in the celebration, including the faithful, as regards the parts that more directly pertain to each.

Since, indeed, many possibilities are provided for choosing the different parts of the Mass, it is necessary for the deacon, the readers, the psalmist, the cantor, the commentator, and the choir to know properly before the celebration the texts that concern each and that are to be used, and it is necessary that nothing be in any sense improvised. For harmonious ordering and carrying out of the rites will greatly help in disposing the faithful for participation in the Eucharist.

This article therefore not only points to the proper choice of the texts for the Mass with a view to the faith community but calls for a joint preparation of the eucharistic celebration. Not only the priest, the readers, and the members of the choir, but also other interested faithful are invited to participate in planning the liturgies, within the possibilities offered by the new Missal, especially the celebrations on Sunday. In this way these liturgies can be truly recognizable common celebrations of Christ's paschal mystery.

Part Two

Active Participation in
the Different Parts of
the Eucharistic Celebration

Introduction

In principle, the new Missal opted for active participation of the lay faithful in the Eucharist. The General Instruction strongly emphasizes this active participation as an integral element of every true eucharistic celebration, thereby ending the one-sided clerical liturgy and paving the way for an ecclesial liturgy, a liturgy of the entire gathered people of God. Yet the question remains whether this principle has been respected consistently in all parts of the renewed eucharistic celebration. We will investigate this in Part Two.

For that research, we obviously follow the *Ordo Missae cum populo*, and take into account the instructions and explanations given by the General Instruction. In particular we will look at the third section of chapter two, the Individual Parts of the Mass (GIRM 46–90), and the first section of chapter four, Mass with a Congregation (GIRM 115–170). In passing, we also refer to other articles of the General Instruction.

Traditionally one saw three parts in the Mass: offertory, consecration, and communion. The so-called Mass of the Catechumens or Fore-Mass preceded these three parts; however, it was not seen as essential. One had fulfilled his or her Sunday obligation if one was present in the church from the offertory on. The new Roman Missal sees two major constituent parts in the eucharistic celebration: the Liturgy of the Word and the Liturgy of the Eucharist. The latter consists of the preparation of the gifts, the eucharistic prayer, and the communion rite. The entire celebration begins with the introductory rites and ends with the concluding rite.

When Christians come together to celebrate the Eucharist, they do this because of the Lord's mandate: "Do this in memory of me" (Luke 22:19). This memorial is a celebration of the paschal mystery of the Lord, of his life, suffering, death, and resurrection, as well as the mission of the Spirit. It is a mandate given to the church, the community of the faithful. This presupposes that the baptized effectively come together to celebrate this memorial. Seen in its biblical context, however, "memorial" means both "to remember" and "to bring something present." In other words, by calling the past events to mind, we also bring them into the present. In this way, we become part of the story and participate in it.

Thus, the eucharistic celebration or memorial service of the Lord should contain two elements: first, the narrative of the Lord's deeds, and then their sacramental actualization, especially in its culmination point: the paschal mystery of Jesus, his total self-surrender for the salvation of all. In other words, word and sacrament are inextricably linked together in the eucharistic celebration. From the beginning, the church has celebrated the Eucharist by making the Lord present in the celebrating community through story and prayer. While invoking the Spirit, the church does in commemoration what the Lord did at the Last Supper around the signs of bread and wine.

When this commemoration of what the Lord did became a more complete Liturgy of the Word preceding the actual Liturgy of the Eucharist cannot be determined with certainty. The fact is that from the middle of the second century onwards a Liturgy of the Word already preceded the Liturgy of the Eucharist.

When we consider the practice of Jesus' meals in the gospels, which were always framed within Jesus' announcement of the coming kingdom of God, Jesus' farewell speech during the Last Supper, the explanation of the Scriptures, and the breaking of the bread in the Emmaus story, then we can understand the bond between the Liturgy of the Word and the Liturgy of the Eucharist in the one eucharistic celebration. This is emphasized by the Constitution on the Sacred Liturgy in article 56, and in loyalty to the oldest tradition of the church: "Do this in memory of me."

Chapter One

The Introductory Rites

Article 46 of the General Instruction gives a summary of the different Introductory rites and their purpose:

> The rites that precede the Liturgy of the Word, namely the Entrance, the Greeting, the Penitential Act, the *Kyrie*, the Gloria in excelsis (Glory to God in the highest) and collect, have the character of a beginning, an introduction, and a preparation.
>
> Their purpose is to ensure that the faithful, who come together as one, establish communion and dispose themselves properly to listen to the Word of God and to celebrate the Eucharist worthily.

In other words, the goal of the introductory rites is twofold: to bring the faithful into communion, and to put them in the proper state for listening to God's Word and for celebrating the Eucharist. The introductory rites not only lead to the Liturgy of the Word, but to the entire eucharistic celebration. The rites want to make the gathered faithful, including the priest, a true community, a liturgical assembly (*assemblée liturgique*), and a conscious people of God. From the beginning, the liturgy presupposes the active participation of all.

Entrance and Entrance Song

The function of the entrance of the priest and his ministers within the assembled group of faithful is to create community awareness. This entrance situates the liturgical assembly in its hierarchical structure. The emphasis of the new Missal on this gathering of the faithful is striking. Article 47 of the General Instruction opens with the words: "When the people are gathered . . . " Article 120, introducing the description of the Mass with a congregation, repeats that phrase: "When the people are gathered . . . " The Order of Mass begins with similar words: "After the people have assembled . . . "

When the priest enters into the congregation, the liturgical assembly is formed and the ecclesia becomes the integral subject of the eucharistic celebration. There is a great difference between the *Ritus servandus* of the Missal of 1570 that started with the words, "The priest who goes to celebrate the Mass . . . " and the Order of Mass, which started with the words, "When the priest is ready he goes to the altar . . . " These words typify the difference between a one-sided clerical liturgy and an ecclesial liturgy.

During the entrance procession, we sing an entrance song. According to article 47 of the General Instruction, this has a fourfold goal: (1) to open the celebration; (2) to foster the unity of the gathered people; (3) to lead their thoughts to the mystery of the liturgical season or feast; and (4) to accompany the entrance of the priest and ministers.

We can interpret the fact that the entrance song should lead to the mystery of the liturgical time or of the feast as an element of active participation, insofar as it presupposes that one participates in the celebration with understanding and insight. There is more, however: article 48 stipulates that the entrance song is done either alternately by the choir and the people, by a cantor and the people, entirely by the people, or by the choir alone. The last possibility holds the danger that the choir will perform rather than invite participation, so that the faithful are deprived of their right to jointly open the celebration. Although attention must be paid to this issue, the description clearly indicates that we may not regard the entrance song as a presidential prayer or a task of the choir, but as a common function of the assembled community.

Originally, the entrance song was an antiphonal song: a psalm that was sung verse after verse, alternately by two choirs or by the choir and the faithful, after first singing a prelude that is now called the antiphon. In the course of time, the emphasis was on the refrain or the antiphon itself, and the number of psalm verses decreased. Additionally, the antiphon usually exposed the theme of the liturgical time or feast.[1]

---

1. Some Sundays were named after the beginning of the Introit, for example, *Gaudete* as the Third Sunday of Advent.

The question is whether it is practically possible for the faithful to sing these antiphons. The Third Instruction for the Implementation of the Constitution of September 3, 1970, already responded to this by stating, "when choosing the songs for the celebration of the Mass, not only its suitability for the local situation and the requirements of the liturgy should be envisaged but also the needs of the faithful who use it."

Based on article 48 of the General Instruction and on what the Latin text says, the USCCB decided:

> In the dioceses of the United States of America there are four options for the Entrance Chant: (1) the antiphon from the Missal or the antiphon with its Psalm from the *Graduale Romanum*, as set to music there or in another setting; (2) the antiphon and Psalm of the *Graduale Simplex* for the liturgical time; (3) a chant from another collection of Psalms and antiphons, approved by the Conference of Bishops or the Diocesan Bishop, including Psalms arranged in responsorial or metrical forms; (4) another liturgical chant that is suited to the sacred action, the day, or the time of year, similarly approved by the Conference of Bishops or the Diocesan Bishop.

These guidelines make it possible for the faithful to participate actively in the entrance song. If the song is well chosen it can indeed introduce the congregation to the specific aspect of the Christ mystery that is celebrated on that day. Perhaps an extra effort will be required to gradually learn to sing these rich antiphons.

Greeting of the Altar and of the People Gathered Together

When the priest reaches the altar, he reverences it with a profound bow and kisses it. He may also incense the cross and the altar. After the entrance song, all together make the sign of the cross. After this, the priest goes to his presidential chair, greets the people, and very briefly introduces them to the Mass of the day.

Greeting of the Altar

The altar is regarded as a symbol of Christ; it is the table around which the Lord's Supper is celebrated. The perfect sacrifice is made present under sacramental signs on this table. The people of God are called together to this table to participate in the Mass. It is the center of the thanksgiving that is accomplished through the Eucharist (compare article 296).

Where the former Missal had a multitude of altar kisses, the Roman Missal reduces this to two: one at the beginning and one at the end of the liturgy, as the first and last act of the priest. This promotes a correct understanding of kissing the altar, that it is an act of faith whereby the priest, on behalf of the assembled community, greets the Lord, who calls us to remember him.

The meaningfulness of the kiss is also clarified by the kiss on the Book of the Gospels. Through the kiss on the altar we venerate the Lord who comes to us in the eucharistic meal, and through the kiss on the Book of the Gospels we venerate the Lord who comes to us in his word.

Yet kissing the altar may not be part of the tradition of Christians in all places. Proof that the renewed liturgy wants to recognize the culture of the people is found in article 273:

> [W]here a sign of this kind is not in harmony with the traditions or the culture of some region, it is for the Conference of Bishops to establish some other sign in its place, with the consent of the Apostolic See.

Sign of the Cross

The renewed liturgy provides that after the entrance song and before the greeting, the priest and all the people together make the sign of the cross. The sign of the cross is a formula that we regularly pronounce when we begin to pray. This Trinitarian formula is an extremely short confession of faith that reminds us of our baptism. When we make the sign of the cross together at the beginning of the eucharistic celebration, we express our belief that we can only celebrate the Eucharist by virtue of our belonging to the church community through our baptism.

Although making a sign of the cross is extremely meaningful at the beginning of the celebration, one might object to its inclusion here. First, when we take the entrance song seriously and see in it the opening of the celebration, as article 47 says, it seems illogical to begin again a ceremony that has already begun. This is doubly the case when the Trinitarian greeting formula is used, "The grace of the Lord Jesus Christ and the love of God and the fellowship of the holy Spirit be with all of you" (2 Cor 13:13) after the sign of the cross. When an entrance song that contains a Gloria to the Father and the Son and the Holy Spirit is sung, the sign of the cross made, and the Trinitarian greeting formula used, we have a threefold repetition of the belief in the Trinity, and a threefold opening of the celebration! We might then ask: when does the Mass actually begin?

These repetitions are clearly the result of a compromise. In its design, *coetus* 10 provided this rubric: when the priest and his assistants reached the altar, they were to perform the required reverence, make a sign of the cross, and stand still for a few moments. Several Synod fathers, however, thought that a solemn sign of the cross made by all at the beginning of the eucharistic celebration should be included. Thus, the sign of the cross was added to the introductory rites.

Greeting of the People Gathered Together

The priest not only greets the altar but also the people gathered together. This is meaningful in its recognition of active participation and should be strongly emphasized. In the previous clerical liturgy, this greeting happened just before an introductory to the collect, after the prayers at the foot of the altar, introit, *Kyrie,* and Gloria, and was not explicit.

The new Missal also accentuates this greeting with two biblical formulations, which can be used in addition to the traditional *Dominus vobiscum,* "The Lord be with you" and *Pax vobis,* "Peace be with you" (when a bishop presides). The first alternate greeting is: "The grace of our Lord Jesus Christ and the love of God and the communion of the Holy Spirit be with you all" (2 Cor 13:13). This greeting points to the Trinitarian dimension of the eucharistic celebration: it is the perfect sacrifice offered to the Father through the priesthood of Christ in the mutual unity of the Holy Spirit. The second formula is the salutation often mentioned in Paul's epistles: "Grace to you and peace from God our Father and the Lord Jesus Christ" (Rom 1:7; 1 Cor 1:3; Gal 1:3; Eph 1:2; Col 1:3; 2 Thess 1:2). Additionally, the traditional greeting, "The Lord be with you," has a biblical origin in Luke 1:28, when the angel greets Mary.

To all these greetings the people respond, *Et cum spiritu tuo,*[2] "And with your spirit." This response is based on Galatians 6:18, "The grace of our Lord Jesus Christ be with your spirit, brothers. Amen." and 2 Timothy 4:22, "The Lord be with your spirit." We find this response first in the *Traditio Apostolico* (Apostolic Tradition), attributed to Hippolytus (ca. 215), more precisely in chapter four with the text of a eucharistic prayer in the ritual of the ordination of a bishop.

There was discussion about the translation of this response. The literal translation of the Latin is "And with your spirit." We think that it is here not, as some thought, a Semitic phrase that would mean "and also with you," but it expresses the recognition that the priest can only perform the sacred action from the Spirit working in him. Thus, in his greeting the priest asks that God's Spirit be with us to participate in the eucharistic celebration and in our response we pray that the spiritual gift he received at his ordination would enable him to fulfill his task as presider over our congregation.

The former ICEL translation preferred to use "and also with you." The Roman Instruction *Liturgiam Authenticam* (March 28, 2001), however, required that "the original text, insofar as possible, must be translated integral and in the most exact manner, without omissions or additions in terms of their content, and without paraphrases or glosses." Accordingly, ICEL prepared a new English translation of the Roman Missal that was approved by the Holy See in April 2010.

This greeting is not only a courtesy but an explicit expression of faith: God's blessing is promised to the assembled faith community, the ecclesia. We declare that the entire eucharistic celebration is a proclamation and an actualization of God's salvation for the faithful. The faithful accept this gratefully and affirmatively. The Eucharist involves the entire community that has gathered by virtue of its baptism. It is an event in which each member of this ecclesia must fully participate. As article 50 says, "By this greeting and the

---

2. The Order of Mass provides a response to the second greeting also: "*Benedictus Deus Pater Domini nostri Iesu Christi,*" "Blessed be God, the Father of our Lord Jesus Christ." Most translations do not make this formula optional and uniformly use "And with your spirit."

people's response, the mystery of the Church gathered together is made manifest" (GIRM 50).

Introductory Words

After the greeting, the priest or another minister may briefly introduce the faithful to the seasonal aspect of the celebration. This is one of the short directives article 35 of the Constitution refers to that should help the faithful participate in the liturgy with more insight. Of course, this introduction should not lead to a homily, but simply evoke the focus of the celebration. We must be aware, however, of repeating the intention of the entrance song, which also should introduce the liturgical time or feast. Article 50 of the Constitution asks to avoid such doublings. It is true that article 50 of the General Instruction says that the priest or another minister *may say* these introduction words, but it is not necessary to say them. With a good entrance song, these introductory words are not needed.

The Penitential Act and the *Kyrie*

Introduction of a Common Penitential Act

After the greeting and the introductory words, if any, the priest invites the assembly to participate in the penitential act, which the entire community carries out through a formula of general confession that concludes with the priest's absolution (GIRM 51). Pope Paul VI referred to the penitential act, or rite of reconciliation with God and brethren, as one of the elements that had suffered injury through accidents of history and was now to be restored to the vigor it had in the days of the holy fathers.[3]

In the Missal of Pope Pius V the penitential act belonged to the prayers at the foot of the altar, and thus to the private prayers of the priest and his ministers. Within the liturgical movement the custom became to say these prayers alternately between priest and faithful, and thus involve the faithful in the penitential act. The new Missal makes the penitential act an integral part of the introductory rites,

---

3. Paulus VI, "Constitutio Apostolica 'Missale Romanum,'" *Notitiae* 5 (1969) 142–146, 144.

which must bring the faithful into the right disposition to participate in the Eucharist.

Three Possible Forms

There are three possible forms for the penitential act. Additionally, on Sundays the Roman Missal also allows the ancient rite of blessing and sprinkling of water that recalls baptism to be performed instead of the penitential act (GIRM 51). When this alternate rite is celebrated, the *Kyrie* is omitted.

Each of the three forms is constructed in the same way: an invitation to take part in the rite, a brief pause for silence, the common praying of the confession, and the priest's absolution. The pause for silence is an opportunity to come to personal repentance or prayer and meets the desire of article 30 in the Constitution, that is, to observe reverent silence at the appropriate time. It is about becoming aware of one's sinfulness, not about a detailed soul-searching. It is also an aspect of active participation: the faithful are invited to associate themselves personally with the common confession.

The first form is the common praying of the *Confiteor*, which is simplified and no longer pronounced first by the priest and then by the faithful. By saying this prayer together, the former distinction between priest and faithful is dropped. The *Kyrie* that follows is clearly seen as an acclamation of Christ, the *Kyrios*.

The second, extremely short form consists of a double invocation of God's mercy, alternately by the priest and the faithful: "Have mercy on us, O Lord / For we have sinned against you. / Show us, O Lord, your mercy / And grant us your salvation." These words are based on Baruch 3:2 and Psalm 85:8. In this case, the subsequent *Kyrie* is also seen as acclamation of Christ. This short form ensures that an extensive introductory rite will not be overloaded, but it is not often used.

The third form consists in praying the *Kyrie* combined with short texts, *invocationes* or "tropes" that precede the acclamations. The Missal itself provides an example, while article 52 of the General Instruction also points to the possibility of using these tropes "by reason of the character of the various languages, as well as of the artistry of the music or of other circumstances." Here the possibility of creativity in the liturgy is given. One can make a connection with the individual aspect of the celebration.

Critical Question

Is this last form, the combination of *Kyrie* and the penitential act, justified? Does it take on too much of a penitential color? Does it not shortchange the *Kyrie*, which of old is an acclamation to Christ, the *Kyrios*? Is it not interpreted as a supplication?

The *Kyrie* seems to have its origin in the East, where it is already mentioned in the fourth century. From there it was passed on to the West. The *Kyrie* was initially prayed after the readings as an acclamation of the people, with a litany and intercessions by the deacon. Gradually the *Kyrie* came to the introductory rite. Under Pope Gregory the Great (papacy 590–604) the diaconal intentions were removed so that only the acclamation prayed by the people remained. Where originally the number of repetitions was dependent on the number of intercessions, it was then given a threefold form: three acclamations that were repeated three times. This threefold prayer gave rise to a Trinitarian interpretation that lasted until recently.[4] From the ninth to the sixteenth century, the practice of introducing tropes into the *Kyrie* was normative. This practice was abolished by the introduction of the Missal of 1570. These tropes were not regarded as a penitential act, but as an extension of the *Kyrie* calls, which at the same time were considered praise and prayers for mercy on behalf of the people.

That the new Missal now sees the *Kyrie* with tropes along with the penitential act is in line with the older tradition. It is therefore wrong to interpret this form of *Kyrie* only as an act of penitence. Above all, the *Kyrie* remains an acclamation, an expression of homage together with a supplication.[5] This means that in the free formulation of these tropes we cannot place the main emphasis on our sinfulness as such, but rather on Christ's work of salvation that liberates people from their sinfulness. This is also evident from the examples given by the Order of Mass: "You were sent to heal the contrite of heart: Lord, have mercy. You came to call sinners: Christ, have mercy. You are

---

4. The reason for this is not only the threefold repetition, but also the addition in Rome of *Christe eleison* to the original *Kyrie eleison*. Because of this, it was obvious to link *Christe eleison* with Christ, and to connect the two *Kyrie eleison* with the Father and, respectively, the Holy Spirit.

5. One thing follows from the other: to honor Christ as the *Kyrios* means the recognition of our own smallness and sinfulness.

seated at the right hand of the Father to intercede for us: Lord, have mercy." This is always a predicate in which a facet of Christ's work of salvation for the benefit of the sins of humankind is expressed. The assembled people can join in acclaiming and supplicating: Lord, have mercy; Christ have mercy.

In practice, however, the *Kyrie* is placed in a penitential context with the combination of the *Kyrie* and the penitential rite. In addition, in translation the *Kyrie* is perceived much less as an acclamation but as a supplication, so that in combination with the penitential act the *Kyrie* totally lost its character as acclamation.

It is a positive sign that the renewed liturgy also sought to renew the age-old tradition by explicitly assigning the *Kyrie* to the people again. Thus, this too became an element of active participation. A single *Kyrie* sung by the choir can be a beautiful artistic event but it is an aberration of the essence of the *Kyrie* as acclamation of Christ-Redeemer by the assembled community of the faithful.

The *Kyrie* can retain its meaning both when it is used separately and when it is used in combination with the penitential act. That is what the General Instruction says in article 52: "After the Penitential Act, the Kyrie, eleison (Lord, have mercy), is always begun, unless it has already been part of the Penitential Act. Since it is a chant by which the faithful acclaim the Lord and implore his mercy, it is usually executed by everyone, that is to say, with the people and with the choir or cantor taking part in it."

In *coetus* 10 there was discussion about the preservation of the *Kyrie* in the introductory rites. The delegates from France wanted to omit the *Kyrie* as an independent prayer in the introductory rites and introduce it as an answer from the faithful to the petitions in the prayer of the faithful. As a result, the introductory rites would be shortened and the doubling, namely, the *Kyrie* in the introductory rites and the *Kyrie* as a response to the intercessions of the prayer of the faithful, would be avoided. Others, especially the German consultors, advocated the preservation of the *Kyrie* because as a familiar refrain it is an important element of active participation. They also pointed out that the *Kyrie* is mainly an acclamation, which can very well come after the greeting of the people.

Moreover, the German consultors saw in the *Kyrie* one of the hymns that belong to the treasure of the sacred music which, according to article 114 of the Constitution, must be preserved and fostered with great care. The majority within the Consilium accepted this statement, but initially decided, in order to avoid overloading the introductory rites, to omit the *Kyrie* in liturgies where the Gloria is sung, as was proposed in the *missa normativa* of 1967.

It may well be that the *Kyrie* in the renewed liturgy of the Eucharist has lost its tension. First, when combined with the penitential act, it loses its acclamation character unless we formulate the tropes in keeping with the examples given by the Order of Mass. Even then, for most of the faithful it will not seem like an homage to the *Kyrios*-Christ. Even when one sings or says the *Kyrie* after the other forms of the penitential act, it does not appear as an acclamation: too much attention goes to the act of penitence so that the *Kyrie* is repressed. We are left with the impression that, on the one hand, the Consilium wanted to give a place to the penitential act in the introductory rites; on the other hand, it dared not touch the place of the *Kyrie*, so that it is left there, but completely lost. It is not an exaggeration to say that the liturgical renewal, even though it explicitly restored the *Kyrie* as an element of active participation, has rather tarnished its purpose.

In hindsight, it may have been more beneficial to place the *Kyrie* at the transition from the Liturgy of the Word to the Liturgy of the Eucharist and connected it with the rite of peace. In response to the message of salvation proclaimed in the Liturgy of the Word and the call for a new way of life, the *Kyrie* would then invite us to reconcile ourselves with God and with each other before celebrating our union in the Liturgy of the Eucharist. This way the *Kyrie* could again have its own place as an acclamation of Christ, the introductory rites would be less cumbersome, and the rite of peace could be integrated more meaningfully.

Gloria

The General Instruction calls the Gloria "a most ancient and venerable hymn by which the Church, gathered together in the Holy Spirit, glorifies and entreats God the Father and the Lamb" (GIRM 53). That is why in *coetus* 10 there were no defenders for the abolition of the Gloria, although together with the entrance song and the *Kyrie* this led to an overload of the introductory rites. The consultors also did not want to accept the proposal to transfer the Gloria as a song of thanks after communion.

Although the *Kyrie* and Gloria have different origins, we can say that the Gloria is a festive reinforcement of the *Kyrie* as homage and supplication. According to the *Sacramentarium Gregorianum,* in the early days of the church the Gloria was only said on Sundays and solemnities, when a bishop presided at the celebration, while the priest was only allowed to say it at Easter. Since the twelfth century, the distinction between bishop and priest began to fade, and the church began to sing the Gloria in any Mass with a somewhat festive character. But the number of holidays in the liturgical year increased greatly in the years following the twelfth century. This meant that the Gloria was sung or prayed nearly every day, and it began to lose its festive nature.

The General Instruction countered this practice by saying that the Gloria "is sung or said on Sundays outside the Seasons of Advent and Lent, and also on Solemnities and Feasts, and at particular celebrations of a more solemn character" (GIRM 53). This is only half a measure, however, since in the celebrations where the people are normally present, namely the Sundays and solemnities, the Gloria falls away only in Advent and Lent. A liturgical catechesis that wants to indicate the festive character of the Gloria will find it difficult to do so with a song that is used in almost every celebration in which the people participate.

The consultors also decided that every time the Gloria is sung the *Kyrie* would be omitted, both in order to shorten the introductory rites and because the Gloria can be interpreted as strengthening the *Kyrie.* The proposed *missa normativa* of 1967 offered a choice: *Kyrie* or Gloria. Later, however, several bishops in the Consilium urged the consultors to keep both. Thus, independent of the will of the consultors, the new Order of Mass has by no means solved the problem of overloading the introductory rites.

A positive step toward active participation was that the General Instruction, following ancient practice, made of the Gloria a hymn that belongs to the entire gathered faithful community.[6] Probably because of the length of the Gloria, the General Instruction provides

---

6. The instruction *De musica sacra et sacra liturgia* (September 3, 1958) had already recommended the singing or reciting of the Gloria, as well as the *Kyrie, Sanctus,* and *Agnus Dei,* by the faithful. Cf. *AAS* 50 (1958) 630–663, p. 640 (n. 25b) and p. 642 (n. 31c). The *Institutio* expressly refers to it as a hymn of the community.

that it can also be sung by the people alternately with the choir, or by the choir alone. If not sung, it is to be recited either by all together or by two parts of the congregation responding one to the other. In several parishes, however, we see the recitation of the Gloria alternating between the priest and the faithful. This distances the priest from the faithful, especially since the Gloria is a hymn that belongs to the celebrating community to which the priest also belongs.

As a personal aside, the Gloria as a hymn must be sung, if possible. If this is not possible it would be better to drop it: little remains of this festive hymn when it is merely rattled off.

The Collect

The introductory rites culminate in the opening prayer that the new Roman Missal calls *collecta* in contrast to the old Missal that spoke of *oratio*. The "new" name comes from the Gallican liturgy and better expresses the meaning of this prayer. The term *oratio* means, in Latin, speech or solemn discourse. Thus, *oratio* in the liturgy means the official prayer of the priest on behalf of the people, who are then invited to pray and to confirm the prayer of the priest. The word *collecta* points out that the priest collects the prayers of the faithful and brings them together into one prayer of the celebrating ecclesia.

Invitation to Pray

The priest can only gather and summarize the prayer of the community when this community is first invited to pray, and effectively given the occasion for personal prayer. Therefore, the General Instruction provides that the priest first invites the faithful to pray through the invitation, "Let us pray." This he says or sings with hands joined. Then he observes a brief silence so that everyone can come to personal prayer.

The invitation "Let us pray," expressed in the plural but in no way a *pluralis majestatis*, indicates that the priest addresses the faithful community to which he himself belongs. All are invited to pray in virtue of their common priesthood. This call only makes sense when time is given for personal prayer and the faithful really can pray. Therefore, it is necessary that a moment of silence be respected by the priest, and that liturgical catechesis points out the meaning of this call and of the moment of silence. Only then is this common prayer offered to the Father by the priest in virtue of his ministerial priesthood through Christ in the Holy Spirit. At that moment, the hierarchically formed liturgical community is actually manifesting itself with the active participation of all, each according to her or his own task.

The Importance of the Amen

The collect also includes the explicit confirmation by the congregation. "The people, joining in this petition, make the prayer their own by means of the acclamation Amen" (GIRM 54). This "Amen" in response to the prayer by the priest is an important element of active participation. In liturgical catechesis, its significance must be explicitly pointed out. Priests and liturgists must strive to ensure that the faithful confirm the "Amen" effectively, and not experience it as simply a closing word. They must affirm their adhesion to what the priest says or asks in their name.

"Amen" is a typical expression of a community that has come together and comes from synagogue worship. In the Old Testament, we find it several times as an expression of the consent of the people, e.g., in 1 Chronicles 16:36 and in Nehemiah 5:13 and 8:6. The Hebrew "Amen" corresponds to the Greek *genoito* and the Latin *fiat*, "May it be." It appears to be an optimal expression of trust in God.

By expressing their "Amen" the faithful people recognize that the prayer pronounced by the presider is their prayer, as well. As *ecclesia* they come to stand in front of the Father, faithfully and in trust directing their prayer to him through Christ in the Holy Spirit.

Presidential Prayer

Through the collect, the priest also clearly exercises his own function within the celebrating faith community. We speak here about the priest's presidential prayers, traditionally said in the *orans* posture. This means that a prayer is offered while standing with the hands extended and lifted upwards. In these presidential prayers, the priest explicitly performs his function by virtue of his ministerial priesthood, that is, to precede the prayer of the people of God. The term "presidential prayer" is a good indication that the priest does not pronounce this prayer separately from the community. This term alone makes it clear that the prayer has little meaning without the explicit and active participation of the faithful, who confirm this by the expressive "Amen" at the end of the prayer. It is precisely in this opening prayer that the priest expressly performs his function of presider for the first time.

Summary and Summit of the Introductory Rites

When we call the opening prayer the collect, it expresses its function as a summary of the previous prayer experience. Similarly, in the course of the eucharistic celebration, we have other such moments of prayer in which the preceding experience is brought to a summarizing climax.

The content of the collect remains fairly general and points to the function of this prayer as a means to bring together the prayer of everyone who belongs to the celebrating community. As such, the consultors who composed the new orations in the Missal took into account the principle of active participation, with an eye toward simplification, truthfulness, and adaptation to the new conditions.

Chapter Two

The Liturgy of the Word

The collect ends the opening rites. Now we are moving on to the first major part of the celebration: the Liturgy of the Word. Here the attention and the center of the action shift from the chair of the priest to the ambo. The word of God and the faithful response of the community are now in the center.

As a result of the biblical movement, the Second Vatican Council, in its first constitution, already underscored the importance of the word of God in the life of the church. The creation of the new Lectionary meets the council's desire. This was not only achieved through a larger number of readings spread over the three years of the Lectionary cycle, but also by offering three readings for each Sunday. This made it possible for the faithful, most of whom exclusively go to church on Sunday, to have a broader exposure to the gospels, the Old Testament, and the apostolic writings.

The General Instruction in article 55 underscores the dialogical structure of the Liturgy of the Word. To speak about dialogue presupposes active participation, here between God and the faithful community:

> For in the readings, as explained by the Homily, God speaks to his people, opening up to them the mystery of redemption and salvation, and offering spiritual nourishment; and Christ himself is present through his word in the midst of the faithful. By their silence and by singing, the people make this divine word their own, and affirm their adherence to it by means of the Profession of Faith; finally, having been nourished by the divine word, the people pour out their

petitions by means of the Universal Prayer for the needs of the whole Church and for the salvation of the whole world.

In these words, we can begin to see a theology of the word, which was noted in the Constitution on the Sacred Liturgy (SC 7). In article 29 of the General Instruction we read:

> When the Sacred Scriptures are read in the Church, God himself speaks to his people, and Christ, present in his own word, proclaims the Gospel.
>
> Therefore, the readings from the Word of God are to be listened to reverently by everyone, for they are an element of greatest importance in the Liturgy.

The word of God is obviously primary in this dialogical structure. This is confirmed by the fact that each of the three readings is concluded by the statement, "The word/Gospel of the Lord," to which the faithful answer, "Thanks be to God/Praise to you, Lord Jesus Christ." On the part of the faithful, this presupposes a willingness not only to listen but also to respond. We do this by making ourselves familiar with the proclaimed word in our prayer, expressing our faith and praying for the salvation for all.

The Readings

The Criteria of the Lectionary and Active Participation

A special *coetus, coetus* 11, worked on the composition of the Lectionary during the years 1964 to 1969. This group consisted of eighteen experts in the liturgical, exegetical, pastoral, and catechetical fields. They started with an inventory of existing lectionaries from the various Eastern and Western rites, including those that dated back to the Reformation. A number of exegetes were asked to indicate a series of pericopes that were suitable as lectures in the liturgy. These texts had to be understandable to the faithful and give them insight into salvation history. With this material, the working group made a list that could be a starting point for the new Lectionary. This list was presented to the Synod of Bishops, along with eight hundred experts, in 1967.

Taking into account the comments of the working group, the Congregation for Divine Worship issued the new *Ordo Lectionum Missae* on May 25, 1969. A second edition was published in 1981. This *Ordo* contained only the list of pericopes. Based on what was presented to the Synod in 1967, the new Lectionary was issued in the years 1970–1972. The Latin *editio typica*, with the texts in full, contains three parts. The current edition published for the United States is normally in four volumes: (1) Sundays and Major Feast Days, Years A, B, C; (2) Weekdays Year I, odd-numbered years, including the feasts of saints with proper readings; (3) Weekdays Year II, even-numbered years, including the feasts of saints with proper readings; and (4) Common of Saints, Rituals, Votives, and Various Needs.

The Arrangement of the Readings on Sundays and Festive Days
There are three principles that govern the composition of the readings for Sundays and festive days: the principle of the three readings, the principle of the three-year cycle, and the principle of thematic harmony during the liturgical seasons.

The first reading, usually from the Old Testament, reflects important themes from the gospel reading. In the Easter Season, however, this reading comes from the Acts of the Apostles. The second reading is from one of Paul's letters or the letters of other apostles. This can also include a reading from the Book of Revelation, depending on the season. The letters are read semi-continuously. The third reading is from the gospels. This arrangement not only offers a more representative portion of the Holy Scripture, it also brings out the unity of the Old and New Testaments and of the history of salvation.

The three-year cycle provides a richer fare for the faithful at the table of God's word. In Year A we read mostly from the Gospel of Matthew. In Year B we read the Gospel of Mark and in the Year C, the Gospel of Luke. The Lectionary editors did not forget the Gospel of John; on the contrary, it may be seen as the most important gospel to the liturgy. A passage from John's gospel is read in all three years during the Easter season, and on the second Sunday in Ordinary Time. Further we read from this gospel on some Sundays in the Years A, B, and C.

Taken all together, this means that in a period of three years we have a great variety of pericopes from the gospels. Provided that the homily is instructive on this count, the faithful can thus become familiar with the characteristics of each of the four evangelists. This arrangement of the Lectionary also shows that the center of gravity lies in the gospel reading.

The third principle is called harmony or semi-continuous reading. Hereabout the *Praenotanda* says:

> The present Order of Readings selects Old Testament texts mainly because of their correlation with New Testament texts read in the same Mass, and particularly with the Gospel text. Harmony of another kind exists between texts of the readings for each Mass during Advent, Lent, and Easter, the seasons that have a distinctive importance or character. In contrast, the Sundays in Ordinary Time do not have a distinctive character. Thus the text of both the apostolic and Gospel readings are arranged in order of semi-continuous reading, whereas the Old Testament reading is harmonized with the Gospel. (67)

There are four different ways to make the correlation between the Old Testament and the gospel reading. First, there is the harmony of citation: when the gospel reading contains a citation from the Old Testament, we read this pericope as the first reading (e.g., the third Sunday of Advent Year A: Matthew 11:2-11 with Isaiah 35:1-6a, 10). Second, there can be a correlation of opposition (e.g., Sixth Sunday in Ordinary Time Year B: Mark 1:40-45 and Leviticus 13:1-2, 45-46). Third, there is the thematic similarity (e.g., Sixth Sunday in Ordinary Time in the Year C: Luke 6:17, 20-26 and Jeremiah 17:5-8). Fourth, there can be a correlation between prediction and fulfillment (e.g., Palm Sunday: the passion narrative and Isaiah 50:4-7). The new Lectionary thus not only offers a broader range of Old Testament readings, but also makes it possible to discover the relationship between Old and New Testaments. A possible criticism, however, is that this method used does not do enough justice to the specific character of the message in the Old Testament and its structure.

The semi-continuous reading of the letters and of the gospels has the advantage of a greater familiarity with the New Testament writing. One disadvantage, though, is that little to no correlation can be made between the second reading and the gospel. This might be seen as somewhat disturbing because of the close correlation between the first reading and the gospel.

Pastoral Principles in Choosing the Readings

The length of the readings was deemed important in creating the Lectionary. People's attention begins to wander when the readings are too long, while too short readings hardly generate any attention. Pastoral considerations opted for a middle ground between too long and too short. These considerations also guided the fact that, for many of the readings, the Lectionary offers a choice between longer and shorter versions.

Texts that present real difficulties are avoided for pastoral reasons. On the one hand, we cannot confront the faithful with texts that raise profound literary, critical, or exegetical problems. On the other hand, we cannot deny them the right to discover the rich content of many of these texts. This is a key difference between an edition of the Bible, which must of course have the full text, and a Lectionary that contains the text in function of the Liturgy of the Word. Nevertheless, we ask here whether a Lectionary that systematically avoids all difficult texts still fulfills its pastoral function. After all, it is never a good method to solve a problem by covering it up. Does requiring that a text should immediately be clear to everyone undermine the specific function of the homily?

For the sake of intelligibility and in order to limit the length of the readings, the Lectionary has omitted a few verses in some pericopes. The preamble justifies this decision not only because they could be unduly long but also "because those readings include some verse that is pastorally less useful or that involves truly difficult questions" (77). While we understand this motivation, we once again ask whether the function of the homily is not undermined here.

Above all, the new Lectionary has more lavishly filled the table of the word for the faithful. In this way, it also meets the desire of Vatican II for more active participation of the faithful. Most especially, it opens up the biblical treasures more widely to the assembled as they celebrate the mysteries of their faith around the eucharistic table.

The Indications of the General Instruction of the Roman Missal and Active Participation

The General Instruction clearly underscores the function of everyone, *in casu* of the deacon and the lector. The priest must no longer silently read the text for himself. Together with and amidst the congregation he also becomes a listener to God's word.[1] The General Instruction calls the reading of the gospel "the high point of the Liturgy of the Word" (GIRM 60).

The faith in and the reverence for the presence of the Lord in his word are expressed in the book from which it is read and the ceremony it is surrounded with. The costly decoration of the Lectionary is traditional and highly justified. To read the gospel from separate sheets of paper with the biblical texts is of little liturgical or biblical insight to the congregation. How can this practice call the faithful to reverence for the word of God? It is also very expressive to use a separate Book of the Gospels or Evangeliary.

During the entrance procession, the lector carries the Lectionary and puts it on the lectern, while the deacon or the priest carries the Book of the Gospels and puts it on the altar. During the singing of the Alleluia, the Book of the Gospels is carried in procession to the lectern. Also, kissing and incensing of the Book of the Gospels express reverence for the presence of Christ in his word.

The active participation of the faithful is expressed by their responses to the readings. The first and second reading end with an expression of faith, "Word of the Lord," while the faithful answer "Thanks be to God." The reading of the gospel even begins with a short dialogue: "The Lord be with you" / "And with your spirit" / "A reading from the holy Gospel according to N." / "Glory to you, O Lord." The deacon or priest ends the reading of the gospel with the words "The Gospel of the Lord" and the faithful answer, "Praise to you, Jesus Christ." We may interpret this answer as an expressive acclamation in which the faithful can actively confess their faith in the presence of the Lord, who speaks to them through his word.

In addition, standing during the reading of the gospel is an active expression of faith. It is important to note that not only the deacon or the priest makes the sign of the cross on the book, then on his forehead, lips, and breast, but the people sign themselves in a similar way. We accept the word with our mind, we confess it with our mouth, and we want to keep it in our heart.

---

1. This was already arranged on September 26, 1964. "Instructio 'Inter oecumenici,'" n. 50: "a qualified reader or the server reads the lessons and epistles with the intervening chants; the celebrant sits and listens." The original draft texts of the then article 34 already called the celebrant a listener to God's word.

The Chants between the Readings

The Responsorial Psalm

The Lectionary provides a responsorial psalm for each first reading. This psalm, especially the response, corresponds to the reading. As a rule, the psalmist or cantor sings or recites the verses of the psalm while the faithful sing or recite the response. When no cantor is available, the lector may recite the verses of the psalm, with the assembly joining in on the response. There are occasions where other psalm texts may be used in place of the responsorial psalm, but in the dioceses of the United States, the USCCB forbids using a song instead of the text of the responsorial psalm (GIRM 61).

The meaning of the responsorial psalm is evident. It expresses the response of the people to the word of God. In this response, the community of the faithful affirms the word of God, that is, the words of encouragement, of hope, of deliverance, of the call to change one's life, and so on. They interiorize the word they have heard in the reading and reformulate it through the biblical psalm. With the right catechesis, the singing of the responsorial psalm should become an important element of active participation. It makes the faithful more aware that God's word appeals to them personally and expects their response (see GIRM 61).

The Alleluia or Gospel Acclamation

Here the General Instruction says:

> a) The Alleluia is sung in every time of year other than Lent. The verses are taken from the Lectionary or the Graduale.
> b) During Lent, instead of the Alleluia, the Verse before the Gospel as given in the Lectionary is sung. It is also possible to sing another Psalm or Tract, as found in the Graduale. (GIRM 62)

The Alleluia functions as an introduction to the reading of the gospel. It differs from the responsorial psalm, which is a reflective answer on the reading that was just heard. The verse before the gospel is a joyful acclamation by which the faithful community welcomes the Lord, who is about to speak to them through the gospel. The Alleluia verse is closely correlated to the reading of the day. Sometimes it is taken from the gospel or it expresses the atmosphere of a feast day. On some Sundays, especially in the great liturgical seasons, the verse is proper to that liturgy. On other Sundays, the verse is chosen from a series of biblical texts.

This Alleluia acclamation is an important element of active participation by which the assembly as a whole welcomes Christ in his word. Therefore, it is important that all sing or repeat the Alleluia that frames the verse, outside of Lent.[2] Conscious and active participation is also expressed when all stand to sing the Alleluia. It is also appropriate to organize the gospel procession, which the Alleluia accompanies, with decorum. Indeed, when the deacon or priest goes to the lectern carrying the Book of the Gospels, slightly elevated, ministers with incense (when used) and candles may accompany him.

The Homily

Beyond the elements that we find in the Lectionary, the Liturgy of the Word also contains the homily, the profession of faith, and the prayer of the faithful. The General Instruction clearly says that the homily is part of the Liturgy of the Word and is strongly recommended, for it is necessary to nurturing the Christian life of the faithful. It also states that the priest should give the homily "standing at the chair or at the ambo itself. . . ." (GIRM 136). As an integral part of the Liturgy of the Word, the sermon no longer begins and ends with the sign of the cross, but follows immediately after the gospel, and is no longer given from the pulpit. The priest celebrant himself should ordinarily give the homily.

The content of the homily should reflect on the readings from Sacred Scripture that the assembly has just heard. It should not be only a kind of exegetical explanation, but above all take an actualizing approach: what does this biblical text mean to us today? The homily also has a liturgical-mystagogic meaning: it can introduce us to the other texts and rites of the celebration in which we participate. The homily must help each person, in his or her own spiritual life, to benefit from the celebration of the mysteries of the faith. The homily in its own way needs to stimulate the prayer of the assembly, to help the faithful on their journey to God and encourage them to engage

---

2. The omission of the Alleluia during Lent clearly serves to emphasize the paschal character of this acclamation.

with the world. Only then can the homily contribute effectively to active participation in the liturgy as the source and summit of a real Christian life.

The communication between preacher and community presupposes that the celebrant himself should ordinarily give the homily. In this way the assembly, to which the priest belongs, can then celebrate in the Liturgy of the Eucharist the salvation that is announced and promised in the Liturgy of the Word. Additionally, this directive makes it clear that the Sunday homily may not be omitted without a serious reason. Finally, as the preceding paragraphs should make clear, the homily is not the time to inform the faithful about the ups and downs of the parish.

The Profession of Faith

After the homily the priest together with the people sing or say the Creed on Sundays and Solemnities (GIRM 68). Through the profession of faith we "may respond to the Word of God proclaimed in the readings taken from Sacred Scripture and explained in the Homily and that they may also honor and confess the great mysteries of the faith by pronouncing the rule of faith in a formula approved for liturgical use and before these mysteries in the Eucharist begins" (GIRM 67).

The Creed is an important element of active participation. Its formulation in the first person singular may promote the personal engagement of all who say it during the celebration. We have two texts of the Creed. The first and oldest one is the so-called Apostles' Creed, and it is written in the singular. The second is the Nicene-Constantinopolitan Creed (325 and 381), usually referred to as simply the Nicene Creed, which was written in the plural. Liturgical use of this Creed has preferred the singular form; however, the Eastern Orthodox and Assyrian churches still use this Creed in the original plural. The use of the singular recalls baptismal language. It echoes the interrogatory form of the profession of faith whereby the candidate for baptism answered "I do" to the questions posed by the minister. Indeed, the candidate for baptism who received this profession of faith during the preparation time (*traditio symboli*) had to learn it by heart and express it at baptism (*redditio symboli*).

From the fourth century on the Roman church has used the *Symbolum Apostolicum*, which is also in the singular. It was called the Apostles' Creed since it was believed that each of the twelve apostles composed an article of the Creed. That is why we also speak about the Twelve Articles of Faith.

The Nicene Creed is an expanded variant of the confession of faith drawn up in a time when the church needed to provide a doctrinal statement of correct belief against controversy, in this case Arianism. With that, the church needed a statement that said, "This is what *we* believe," which is why this Creed was written in the plural.

The Roman church long resisted incorporating the Nicene Creed into the eucharistic celebration. It was not until the eleventh century that Rome accepted it under pressure from the German Emperor Henry II. The Nicene Creed had first spread in Spain with the Council of Toledo in 589, when the Visigoths renounced Arianism, and from 784, among the Carolingians in Germany and Gaul. Rome's hesitation with adopting this Creed in the liturgy was related to the use of the Apostles' Creed in baptismal liturgy: for Rome the Creed was an element in the baptismal liturgy, not in the eucharistic celebration.

Once the Creed had its place in the Mass, it was possible to give it an important meaning in loyalty to its origin. It is precisely by virtue of our baptism that we are able to celebrate the Eucharist. Therefore, when we celebrate the Eucharist on Sundays and Solemnities, the profession of faith is an explicit baptismal memory. We are aware and express solemnly that we belong to the priestly and royal people of God. We recognize that we came together to remember God's wonderful work of salvation, to celebrate our union with God, and to worship him through Christ in the Holy Spirit.

Nevertheless, we can ask whether or not we are dealing with repetition here. The Creed is a profession of our faith, but isn't the fact that we celebrate the Eucharist already a profession of our faith? In each eucharistic celebration we say, "When we eat this bread and drink this cup, we proclaim your death, O Lord, until you come in glory." Further, is the eucharistic prayer not a celebration of the mysteries of faith, a grateful confession of the entire history of salvation? Less in the old Roman Canon, but more so in the new eucharistic prayers this intention comes to the fore.

The fourth eucharistic prayer especially is one of remembrance and thanksgiving for salvation history, starting with creation. Are we willing to omit the Creed on Sundays when we use the fourth eucharistic prayer? In this way, all our attention might go to this beautiful summary of salvation history. And yet we have to underscore that the eucharistic prayer belongs to the presidential prayers of the priest, while reciting the Creed can be an important element of active participation. In this sense, we have to conclude that there is no repetition.

In order to make the profession of faith truly an element of active participation it is necessary to be aware of what we actually say in this profession. The weekly recitation of either Creed can lead to routine recitation, however, so that all attention to its content disappears and we can hardly speak about conscious, active participation. We might prevent this by only praying the Creed a few times a year, which may lead to a conscious and active profession of faith by the celebrating community.

The recitation of the Nicene Creed or *a fortiori*, singing it takes a certain amount of time, so that the smooth transition from the readings to the intercessions is somewhat disturbed. The use of the shorter Apostles' Creed could solve this problem. During the Synod of Bishops in 1967 one of the papal queries was, "Should authority be given to the conferences of bishops to use the Apostles' Creed as well as the Nicene Creed in the Mass?" Of the 183 fathers voting, 142 said yes. Afterwards, the Congregation for Divine Worship allowed the use of the two Creeds every time a conference of bishops asked for it, as the Belgian conference of bishops did. The *Directory for Masses with Children* (November 1, 1973) stated, "If the Profession of Faith occurs at the end of the liturgy of the word, the Apostles' Creed may be used with children, especially because it is part of their catechetical formation (no. 49). It is urged, moreover, that children should become accustomed to the Nicene Creed little by little, the right to use the Apostles' Creed indicated in no. 49 remaining intact." Since the 2002 edition, the Apostles' Creed is included in the Roman Missal with the indication, "Instead of the Nicene-Constantinopolitan Creed, especially during Lent and Easter time, the baptismal Symbol of the Roman Church, known as the Apostles' Creed, may be used."

Although the Latin of the Nicene-Constantinopolitan Creed in the eucharistic celebration is in the singular, until recently the plural was used in English. Other languages kept the singular. The new English translation of the Roman Missal returned to the traditional use and changed some words in order to make the prayer closer to the Latin text. It would be helpful to discuss these nuances in our liturgical catechesis.

The Prayer of the Faithful

Significance

The final element of the Liturgy of the Word is the prayer of the faithful, or universal prayer. This is one of the parts of the Mass that, "lost through the vicissitudes of history are to be restored according to the ancient tradition of the holy Fathers, as may seem appropriate or necessary" (SC 50).

The prayer goes back to the earliest Christian times. Already Paul said, "First of all, then, I ask that supplications, prayers, petitions, and thanksgivings be offered for everyone, for kings and for all in authority, that we may lead a quiet and tranquil life in all devotion and dignity. This is good and pleasing to God our savior, who wills everyone to be saved and to come to knowledge of the truth" (1 Tim 2:1-4). Clemens, Justin, and Hippolytus, and thereafter several church fathers in their writings mentioned the *oratio communis,* or common prayer, as part of the liturgy. Justin, for example, mentions that the newly baptized were brought to the assembly "in order that we may offer hearty prayers in common for ourselves and for the illuminated persons, and for all others in every place."[3] He also writes that on Sundays after the homily "we all stand up together and send up prayers."[4] In the West, the *oratio fidelium,* or prayer of the faithful disappeared from the liturgy of the Mass around the middle of the sixth century (except on Good Friday).

Under the impetus of the liturgical movement, many worked for the reintroduction of the *oratio fidelium.* They saw in it an important

---

3. Justinus, "Apologia I," c. 65, *PG* 6, k. 429–430.
4. Ibid., c. 67.

element of active participation.[5] The renewed liturgy of the eucharistic celebration restored the universal prayer to its original place in the liturgy and underscored its importance for active participation (GIRM 69). In fact, the introduction of this prayer had already happened through the instruction *Inter Oecumenici* of September 26, 1964. The General Instruction qualifies the common praying of the *oratio universalis* as exercising the office of the baptismal priesthood of the faithful.

A Doubling?

Does the universal prayer repeat what is said in the *Kyrie* and the *mementoes* of the eucharistic prayer? The *Kyrie* is in the first place an acclamation of Christ, the *Kyrios*. When combined with the penitential act, there is no duplication with the universal prayer. In this case, the *Kyrie* is above all a confession of Christ's salvation work on behalf of sinful humanity. By the universal prayer, however, the faithful fulfill their role as priestly people to pray for the needs of the church and the world.

The prayer of the faithful is not a repetition of the *mementoes* either. The *mementoes* are about certain persons, living or dead, who are mentioned *nominatim*, by name. The universal prayer is about general intentions that transcend the individual intentions of the faithful present in the celebration. In French, they justly speak about *prière universelle*, universal prayer.

A second difference between the prayer of the faithful and the *mementoes* lies in the priesthood that establishes them. The *mementoes* belong to the presidential prayers during the eucharistic prayer. They come into being by virtue of the ministerial priesthood that of course is not isolated from the faithful community over which the priest presides. The universal prayer, however, is typically the prayer of the entire assembly as the people of God, by virtue of their baptismal priesthood. Although the priest begins this prayer with a brief introduction and concludes it with a prayer, it belongs to the

---

5. For example, during the liturgical congress of Maria Laach (Germany) in 1951 J.A. Jungmann and P.M. Gy were advocates for this reintroduction. Cf. Pierre-Marie Gy, *"Signification pastorale des prières du prône,"* *La Maison-Dieu* 30 (1952) 125–136.

community. In the introduction the priest invites the faithful to pray; with the concluding prayer he asks God to accept the intentions. As in the opening prayer before the Liturgy of the Word, in this concluding prayer the priest collects the universal intentions of the celebrating community.

The Prayer of the Faithful as Bridge

The concluding prayer of the prayer of the faithful functions as the concluding prayer of the entire Liturgy of the Word. In this way, it is a bridge to the Liturgy of the Eucharist. Having listened to the word of God and the development of his plan of salvation, we dare to stand before God to present him with the needs of the whole church and the world. With regard to active participation, the universal prayer is also the summit of the Liturgy of the Word.

The prayer of the faithful leads to the Liturgy of the Eucharist, where the mystery of salvation culminating in Christ's paschal mystery becomes present in our celebration. There we enter into communion with the Lord who calls us and strengthens us to build the humane world we are praying for. Since the universal prayer has such an eminent significance for active participation, it is important to emphasize this in our liturgical catechesis.

Content of the Prayer of the Faithful

About the content of the prayer of the faithful, we refer to the four kinds of intentions, mentioned in the General Instruction (GIRM 70).[6] The first series deals with the general interests and needs of the church, e.g., the unity of Christians, the missions, priestly vocations, the episcopal and papal monthly intentions, and so on. The second category deals more precisely with secular needs such as peace, jus-

---

6. Compare SC 53. The text of the scheme presented at the council was literally inspired by 1 Timothy 2:1-2. The formulation "and all who are in high positions" bumped into the fierce opposition from Bishop Pildàin y Zapiàin who made a plea for the poor in the church (*Acta Synodalia*, Vol. I, pars. II, 156–158, 156). The commission decided to change this into "*pro iis qui nos in potestate regunt*" as in the renewed paschal vigil, where this way the intercession for the emperor was changed, and into "*pro iis qui variis premuntur necessitatibus.*" A proposal of another bishop added "*ac pro omnibus hominibus totiusque mundi salute*" (*Acta Synodalia*, Vol. I, pars. II, p. 302).

tice, tolerance, cooperation, dealing with economic crisis, rulers over the people,[7] and so on. In the third series of intentions we pray for all who are suffering: illness, loneliness, people who suffer from war and violence, from poverty or underdevelopment, refugees, and prisoners. The fourth group of intentions are local needs, not so much what concerns individuals but the parish community as a whole.

Through the intentions in the prayer of the faithful, it becomes clear that the church is not acting as an organization removed from the world. On the contrary, through action and prayer the church wants to work both in this world and for this world. Here the church shows, specifically in the shape of the local community, how it wants to work on the *consecratio mundi*. Here it becomes clear that the church is "a sacrament—a sign and instrument, that is, of communion with God and of the unity of the whole human race" (LG 1).

---

7. In so far as their task is to lead the people for whom they are responsible to a decent human existence. Compare the Latin text "*pro rem publicam moderantibus et salute totius mundi.*"

Chapter Three

The Liturgy of the Eucharist

The Liturgy of the Eucharist consists of three parts: the preparation of the gifts, the eucharistic prayer, and communion. The General Instruction of the Roman Missal points to the connection between these parts and establishes the link between the Liturgy of the Eucharist and Jesus' actions during the Last Supper:

> At the Last Supper Christ instituted the Paschal Sacrifice and banquet, by which the Sacrifice of the Cross is continuously made present in the Church whenever the Priest, representing Christ the Lord, carries out what the Lord himself did and handed over to his disciples to be done in his memory.
>
> For Christ took the bread and the chalice, gave thanks, broke the bread and gave it to his disciples, saying: Take, eat and drink: this is my Body; this is the chalice of my Blood. Do this in memory of me. Hence, the Church has arranged the entire celebration of the Liturgy of the Eucharist in parts corresponding to precisely these words and actions of Christ, namely:
>
> a) At the Preparation of the Gifts, the bread and the wine with water are brought to the altar, the same elements, that is to say, which Christ took into his hands.
>
> b) In the Eucharistic Prayer, thanks is given to God for the whole work of salvation, and the offerings become the Body and Blood of Christ.
>
> c) Through the fraction and through Communion, the faithful, though many, receive from the one bread the Lord's Body and from the one chalice the Lord's Blood in the same way the Apostles received them from the hands of Christ himself. (GIRM 72)

Preparation of the Gifts

An Important Remark

A remarkable change from the previous Missal is the name of the first part of the Liturgy of the Eucharist. We no longer speak about the offertory, but about the preparation of the gifts. The intention in making this change was to bring more clarity to a rite that was overloaded in the course of time and often misunderstood.

In the earliest Christian communities the offertory was purely a functional act: bringing the gifts to the altar so the eucharistic prayer could be pronounced over them. This is what Justin Martyr (100–165) says in his first *Apologia* (ca. 150):

> And on the day called of the Sun all who live in cities or in the country gather together to one place, and the memoirs of the apostles or the writings of the prophets are read for long as time allows. Then, when the reader has ceased, the president in a discourse makes an admonition for the imitation of these good things. Then we all rise together and send up prayers. And as we said before, when we have finished our prayer, bread and wine and water are brought, and the president in like manner sends up prayers and thanksgivings, according to his ability, and the people assent, saying Amen. And there is a distribution to each, and a participation of that over which thanks have been given. And to those who are absent a portion is sent through the deacons. And they who are well to do, and willing, give what each thinks fit. And what is collected is deposited with the president. And he provides for the orphans and widows and those in need through sickness or through other cause, and those who are in prison, and the strangers sojourning among us, and in a word takes care of all who are in want.[1]

Hippolytus, in his *Traditio Apostolico* (ca. 215), speaks about the deacons and the newly baptized bringing the gifts to the altar during the eucharistic celebration.[2] In the time of Cyprian of Carthage (ca. 200–258) it seemed that the norm was for the faithful to bring

---

1. Justinus, *Apologia* I, c. 67, *PG* 6, k. 429–430.
2. Bernard Botte, *Hippolyte de Rome. La Tradition Apostolique d'après les anciennes versions. Introduction, traduction et notes.* Sources chrétiennes 11bis (Paris, 1968²) 90–91.

the gifts to church, and he criticizes the wealthy for coming to the Lord's Supper without a gift and hence taking a part of the gifts that the poor have brought.[3]

A difference arose between East and West about the place of the faithful bringing the gifts. In the East, but also in the Gallic-Frankish church, the people brought their gifts to a side space of the church, the *sacrarium* (sacristy), before the beginning of the celebration. From there, at the precise moment of the offertory, the ministers brought the bread and wine in a procession to the altar. In the East that practice has survived in the Great Entrance.

In the churches of North Africa, Milan, and Rome (and possibly Spain) the presentation of gifts by the faithful received a place in the celebration itself. At the moment of the preparation of the gifts they could present their gifts to the priest, who took from those gifts the bread and wine he needed for the Eucharist. In the *Ordo Romanus I* we find a description of the offertory rite during the seventh century. It was a great procession of the aristocracy to the pope and of the faithful to his assistants to present their gifts. The gifts of bread and wine necessary for the Eucharist were placed on the altar by the deacon, the gifts of the pope were added to them, and the remaining gifts were used for the sustenance of the clergy and the poor.[4]

After the importation of the Roman liturgy into the Frankish regions, the church began to organize a procession by the faithful who brought the gifts to the altar. In addition to bread and wine, other gifts were brought forward. This practice changed during the Middle Ages, when the church began to use unleavened bread for the communion hosts. With that, the gifts of bread and wine presented by the faithful were no longer consecrated and put on the altar. The offertory procession remained for a while but it no longer had a connection with presenting the gifts intended for the consecration. Other gifts were still presented, however, including money. This practice developed into the monetary collection and Mass stipends, losing the original meaning of the offertory rite. The

3. Cyprianus, "Liber de opere et eleemosynis," c. 15, *PL* 4, k. 612–613.
4. Michel Andrieu, *Les Ordines Romani du haut Moyen Age*, part II (Louvain, 1948) 90–95.

Missal of Pope Pius V does not even speak about the presentation of the gifts by the faithful.

The liturgy-historical works of the previous century rediscovered this rite and the liturgical movement considered it an important element of active participation.[5] The sacrifice of the church can only happen during the eucharistic prayer when the gifts of bread and wine, by the invocation of the Holy Spirit and the words of institution, have become the Body and Blood of Jesus Christ. Because the presentation of the gifts cannot be understood as bringing our own sacrifice to the altar, it can be seen as the expression of our fundamental receptivity to God's gift of the Eucharist. Equally we may see it as an expression of our desire to participate in the sacrifice of Christ. In this sense, this rite is more than simply preparing the table.

The accompanying prayers of the previous Missal could easily lead to a misunderstanding of the unique and correct sacrificial moment in the eucharistic celebration. One could even speak about the "little Canon," for example, the *Suscipe* at the presentation of the bread: "Accept, O holy Father, almighty and eternal God, this unspotted host, which I, Thy unworthy servant, offer unto Thee, my living and true God, for my innumerable sins . . . " and the *Offerimus* at the presentation of the wine: "We offer unto Thee, O Lord, the chalice of salvation, beseeching Thy clemency, that it may ascend before Thy divine Majesty, as a sweet savor, for our salvation, and for that of the whole world." It seems as if here we have already the *oblatio* of the eucharistic prayer. See also the *Veni Sancta Trinitas* that shows kinship with the epiclesis, and the *Suscipe Sancta Trinitas* that is reminiscent of the anamnesis and the intercessions. The fact that the priest had to lift up the paten with the host and the chalice also led to a misunderstanding of the rite.

Where initially the preparatory commission for the revision of the Order of Mass preferred to omit the accompanying prayers and to reduce the rite to a simple presentation of bread and wine, which was then placed on the altar, under the pressure of the Consilium and the Synod of Bishops of 1967, an intermediate solution was chosen.

---

5. Already in 1921, Dom Lambert Beauduin (1873–1960) drew attention to this rite. Lambert Beauduin, "L'Offertoire jadis et aujourd'hui," *Questions Liturgiques et Paroissiales* 6 (1921) 30–45.

The Consilium searched for a few short texts, in which every allusion to an independent sacrificial character of this rite was avoided. It became a combination of a few Jewish meal prayers that praise God for the fruits of creation, and an allusion to human labor through which bread and wine are created. Next to the accompanying chant and the prayer over the gifts, the washing of the hands and the *Orate fratres* were kept. We will now investigate the rite of the preparation of the gifts in so far it promotes simplicity, understanding, and active participation of the faithful.

The Bringing Forward of the Gifts

Article 73 of the General Instruction says:

> At the beginning of the Liturgy of the Eucharist the gifts which will become Christ's Body and Blood are brought to the altar.
>
> First of all, the altar or the Lord's table, which is the center of the whole Liturgy of the Eucharist, is made ready when on it are placed the corporal, purificator, Missal, and chalice (unless this last is prepared at the credence table).

This way it becomes clear that at this moment the Liturgy of the Eucharist begins. During the Liturgy of the Word the ambo or the chair of the priest were the center of the liturgical action. This now shifts to the altar. In celebrations with the assistance of a deacon, he prepares the altar. If no deacon is present, the acolyte places the corporal, the purificator, the chalice, the pall, and the Missal on the altar. In the meantime the priest remains at the chair (GIRM 178, 190).

The General Instruction praises the practice of the faithful presenting the gifts of bread and wine:

> The offerings are then brought forward. It is a praiseworthy practice for the bread and wine to be presented by the faithful. They are then accepted at an appropriate place by the Priest or the Deacon and carried to the altar. Even though the faithful no longer bring from their own possessions the bread and wine intended for the liturgy as was once the case, nevertheless the rite of carrying up the offerings still keeps its spiritual efficacy and significance. Even money or other gifts for the poor or for the Church, brought by the faithful or collected in the church, are acceptable; given their purpose, they are to be put in a suitable place away from the Eucharistic table. (73)

This procession with the gifts, here indicated as a praiseworthy but not mandatory rite, thus corresponds to an old tradition. The liturgical movement that interpreted this rite as an element of active participation had been zealous for its re-introduction. At times in the past, the significance of this rite had been a bit exaggerated and misunderstood, such as with bringing forward work tools that after the celebration were taken home again. The re-introduction of the rite would need to present it in its most simple and direct form.

Today the renewed eucharistic liturgy sees, in the bringing forward of gifts by the faithful, an element of active participation:

> It is desirable that the participation of the faithful be expressed by an offering, whether of the bread and wine for the celebration of the Eucharist or of other gifts to relieve the needs of the Church and of the poor. (GIRM 140)

On the other hand, one also sees the difficulties in a correct interpretation of this rite. First, people no longer bring bread and wine from home with them. The priest himself takes care of that. The event could seem rather comical: the priest makes bread and wine available to the faithful so that they can deliver it back to him. As such, nothing is left of the original rite except the act of bringing forward. We can point here to the monetary collection: part of it is used for the purchase of bread and wine, so in that sense, these gifts directly come from the community. More than that, however, the new Missal sees a spiritual significance in the act of bringing forward. By the presentation of the gifts that become the actual signs of Christ's total self-giving, his Body and Blood, the people of God express their willingness to participate in this offering. In our liturgical catechesis to bring the faithful to active participation, we must highlight this aspect of the presentation of gifts.

The General Instruction makes a clear distinction between the gifts needed for the Eucharist and other gifts, such as those for the needs of the poor, the maintenance of the church building, the problems of the world, and so on. These are to be put in a suitable place near the eucharistic table. These gifts have a pronounced charitable character and are not objects that are then taken away. These gifts are not essential for the realization of the Eucharist, but they can show our willingness to join Christ's paschal sacrifice. They help make the connection between the celebration of the Christian covenant of love in the Eucharist and the love we express through our commitment to a better world.

With respect to the bread that is presented, it is meaningful to point out to the faithful that the host for the priest and the hosts for the faithful lie on the same paten. "For the Consecration of hosts, a large paten may fittingly be used, on which is placed the bread both for the Priest and the Deacon and also for the other ministers and for the faithful" (GIRM 331). Previously the paten was a small plate on which only the host for the priest lay. There may also be some larger hosts that can be broken during the fraction rite and given to the faithful. This way the faithful can feel that they actively participate in the one consecrated bread.

The Accompanying Chant

Article 74 of the General Instruction refers to the offertory chant that accompanies the presentation of the gifts. This chant originated in the church of North Africa at the time of Augustine of Hippo (354–430). Initially it was an extensive song that included an antiphon and psalm. In the Missal of 1570, when the procession with the gifts no longer existed, only the antiphon remained. The new Missal does not even provide a verse for the presentation of the gifts, which means this song does not belong to the ritual. It is only an accompaniment to the procession and is only meaningful when a procession is effectively organized. A moment of silence or some gentle organ music may be more suitable. If no song is chosen the priest may say the accompanying prayers in an audible voice, to which the faithful respond, "Blessed be God for ever."

Prayers Accompanying the Preparation of the Gifts

In the articles 141 and 142 the General Instruction describes the following action:

> The Priest accepts the paten with the bread at the altar, holds it slightly raised above the altar with both hands and says quietly, Benedictus es, Domine (Blessed are you, Lord God). Then he places the paten with the bread on the corporal.

After this, as the minister presents the cruets, the Priest stands at the side of the altar and pours wine and a little water into the chalice, saying quietly, Per huius aquae (By the mystery of this water). He returns to the middle of the altar and with both hands raises the chalice a little, and says quietly, Benedictus es, Domine (Blessed are you, Lord God). Then he places the chalice on the corporal and, if appropriate, covers it with a pall.

We find these prayers in the Order of Mass:

> Blessed are you, Lord, God of all creation. Through your goodness we have this bread to offer, which earth has given and human hands have made. It will become for us the bread of life.
> By the mystery of this water and wine may we come to share in the divinity of Christ, who humbled himself to share in our humanity.
> Blessed are you, Lord, God of all creation. Through your goodness we have this wine to offer, fruit of the vine and work of human hands. It will become our spiritual drink.

After the idea to place bread and wine on the altar was rejected, some adapted sentences from the *Didache* were proposed within the Consilium. About the bread: "Just as the bread was first scattered, then was gathered and became one, so let your Church be gathered into your kingdom. Glory be yours, God, in eternity." About the wine: "You, Lord, have created all things and have given drink to the children of men for their enjoyment. Give us the spiritual drink that leads to eternal life. Glory be yours, God, in eternity." In the end, these became the quoted prayers, which are a combination of the Jewish *birkat*, which praises God for the gifts of his creation, and of a reference to human labor, through which the gifts come into being.

In the *missa normativa* celebrated during the Synod of Bishops on October 24, 1967 the Consilium proposed that the accompanying prayers would only be said *pro opportunitate*, if they were deemed necessary. When the amendments were tabled, however, it was asked that the prayers be mandatory.[6] This was apparently taken into account. The Missal states that in the case of not singing, the priest *may* say these prayers in an audible voice. The priest can therefore judge

---

6. Cf. X., "De Liturgia in primo Synodo episcoporum," *o.c.*, 358.

whether it is more favorable in a pastoral sense to say these prayers in silence or to pray them in an audible voice, *with* the acclamations by the faithful. At first glance, one might be happy about this and say it is another element of active participation. Yet we may wonder whether this acclamation is useful in the context of the preparation of the gifts.

Although we can offer criticism about the usefulness of these prayers, which are also called "private prayers," we can also point to their rich content. In them we glorify God as the creator who gives us what we need to live. In this sense, bread and wine represent God's creation. But God calls us to expand this creation in a human way through our work. In this sense, bread and wine also represent our work. Therefore, we also glorify God. Even more, we bring bread and wine that include both God's creation and our labor, so that through the eucharistic prayer they will become the sacrificed Body and Blood of Christ. As such, the bread and wine are not separate from their original meaning.

When Christ's Body and Blood feed us in the signs of bread and wine, we can thank God for all his gifts. Beginning with creation and our cooperation in it, these gifts come to a culmination in the redeeming self-surrender of God's Son, Jesus Christ, our Lord. This strengthens our commitment to the salvation of the world. Under the impulse of the unifying Spirit, we will thus become more and more the ecclesial Body of Christ on earth.

For many of the faithful, the prayers accompanying the presentation of the gifts will continue to evoke the idea of sacrifice. An appropriate catechesis can be helpful here. Nevertheless, the question remains about whether or not the principle that the Consilium had in mind when it started with the renewal of this rite has been understood, namely, that the prayers and ritual of the presentation of the gifts deserve a fundamental revision in order to better express the significance of this rite so the faithful can more easily understand it.

That the revised rite continues to evoke the idea of sacrifice is strengthened by the ritual action of the priest when he holds the paten then the chalice slightly raised above the altar during the prayers. Indeed, the difference in the rubrics when compared to the former ritual action is evident. Before the rubrics for the priest read, *offerens patenam (calicem)* and today, *aliquantulum elevatum.*

Every allusion to *offere* is omitted in the terminology. But the faithful usually do not read the rubrics. They see that the paten and chalice are raised above the altar, which evokes the idea of offering—more so because some priests continue to make an ample gesture of offering.

An appropriate catechesis of this ritual might return to the institution narratives and connect them with the Jewish table prayers, where the father, during the prayer of thanksgiving, holds bread and chalice slightly raised above the table. We, however, say our prayer of thanksgiving during the eucharistic prayer. Then it makes sense to elevate the gifts that have become the Body and Blood of Christ, although not separate from their natural origin. That is why this elevation during the preparation of the gifts, with its allusion to an offering, is an undesirable repetition.

Many of the faithful may not understand why the priest not only pours wine into the chalice, but also a little water.[7] Originally, this rite had a practical reason that later received a symbolic significance. In the early days of Christianity Jews, Greeks, and Romans had to dilute their heady wine with a little water in order to make it drinkable. Already by the second century, one interpreted this as a symbol of the union of the divine and human nature in Christ. Further, it also could be interpreted as a symbol of the union of the faithful with Christ. Indeed, once the wine is diluted with the water it can no longer be separated: it is an indissoluble union.

The accompanying prayer during this blending comes from the Christmas *oratio* of Pope Leo the Great (papacy 440–461). The text in the new Missal, shorter than before, is as follows: "By the mystery of this water and wine may we come to share in the divinity of Christ, who humbled himself to share in our humanity." As before, the priest says this prayer in silence. So where is the understanding for the faithful?

Even if one reads the text in the Missal, it creates a lot of confusion for anyone not aware of the historical-dogmatic background

---

7. According to the *Ordo Romanus I* the choir, which could not take part in the procession with the gifts, expressed their participation by giving water to the subdeacon, who then gave it to the archdeacon who poured the water into the chalice in the form of a cross. Subsequently this was interpreted as a blessing. "*Deinde descendit subdiaconus sequens in scholam, accipit fontem de manu archiparaphonistae et defert archidiacono, et ille infundit faciens crucem in calice,*" OR I, 66.

of the ritual. It is not through the mystery of water and wine that we share in the divinity, but through our participation in the eucharistic sacrifice. It can only be a symbolic indication of our sharing in the divinity through our sacramental union with Christ that began through our baptism.

Most likely the rite of mixing the water and wine has been retained for the sake of the historical-dogmatic background. Against the Monophysites—who rejected the addition of water to the wine because they believed that in the person of Jesus Christ there was only one, divine nature rather than two natures, divine and human—the Council of Florence in 1438, which aimed for union with the Eastern Rite churches, ordered the addition of water to the wine. Martin Luther rejected this mixture in so far as it referred to our union with Christ, whereby the church was offered together with Christ in the Mass, because it would destroy the uniquely divine work. The Council of Trent responded to this by explicitly demanding the addition of water to the wine.[8]

Because of this theological, historical-dogmatic background, the mixture of water and wine is maintained. With regard to understanding the reason for this rite, it might be better to mix the water with the wine before the eucharistic celebration begins. The new Order of Mass speaks about "a little water." Since the late Middle Ages, this practice has given rise to all sorts of sentimental and individualistic ideas of devotion, such as, "this little drop is my little offering that is taken up in Christ's great sacrifice." A clarifying catechesis is again required here.

Then the priest replaces the chalice on the corporal, bows, and says quietly "With humble spirit and a contrite heart may we be accepted by you, O Lord, and may our sacrifice in your sight this day be pleasing to you, Lord God." Apparently, this prayer has been retained

---

8. "The holy council in the next place calls to mind that the Church has instructed priests to mix water with the wine that is to be offered in the chalice. Because it is believed that Christ the Lord did this, and also because from His side there came blood and water; the memory of this mystery is renewed by this mixture, and since in the Apocalypse of St. John the 'people' are called 'waters,' the union of the faithful people with Christ their head is represented." *Conc. Trid.*, Sessio XXII, chapter VII.

because of its meaning as a demand for the union of our self-giving with Christ's. As a church community we are going to offer Christ's sacrifice to the Father and we ask him to accept our self-giving along with this sacrifice. Again, we wonder if this is the moment for such a prayer. Does it not rather belong to the eucharistic prayer? Is it not another relic of the former offertory rite as a "little Canon"? In addition, the priest also says this prayer quietly. Does this prayer belong to a period in which the Mass more resembled a personal exercise of the priest's devotion, in which the faithful might be present to edify their own devotion, rather than the common celebration of the assembled people of God?

The Incensing of the Altar

The new Order of Mass no longer provides an accompanying prayer during the incensing of the altar. This rite, which was once mandatory in a solemn Mass, is no longer an obligation. We are dealing here with a pastoral motive: wherever this rite can be experienced as meaningful, it can be performed. In those places where it seems meaningful, no explanatory prayer needs to be added. To avoid repetition it is not necessary to incense the altar again when this was already done during the introductory rites.

The Washing of the Hands

> After the prayer In spiritu humilitatis (With humble spirit) or after the incensation, the Priest washes his hands standing at the side of the altar and, as the minister pours the water, says quietly, Lava me, Domine (Wash me, O Lord). (GIRM 145)

What the priest has to say here is much more concise than in the former Missal.

The washing of the hands has a very old liturgical meaning that goes back to the Jewish Passover meal, where there were ritual washings of the hands. Although a practical meaning of this rite, which comes after the preparation of the gifts and the incensation, can be defended, the handwashing seems to have had a symbolic meaning from the beginning. Both Hippolytus and Tertullian already mention it, and the explanation of Cyril of Jerusalem in the fourth century is convincing:

. . . the ablution is a symbol of our obligation to be clean from all sins and transgressions. The hands symbolize action. So by washing them we signify plainly the purity and blamelessness of our conduct.[9]

In Western tradition, there were several moments of handwashing in the Liturgy of the Eucharist, accompanied or not with prayer texts. Eventually, the Missal of Pope Pius V prescribed the handwashing in the place where it still stands and accompanied by Psalm 26:6.[10] At the time of Pope Pius V the procession with the gifts no longer existed, so that if the handwashing would have been associated with it at some point, all the attention now went to its symbolic meaning.

In the preparation of the renewed liturgy, some were in favor of abolishing the washing of hands, or to preserve this rite only after an effective presentation of the gifts and incensation. A reference to the text of Cyril of Jerusalem, in which the symbolic meaning was emphasized, was decisive for the preservation of the rite. If one does not want to give a practical meaning to it, would it not be better to do the handwashing before the gifts are brought forward, so that when the priest has placed the gifts on the altar, he can immediately pronounce the prayer over the gifts? We would then have a meaningful succession: through the washing of hands we express our desire for inner purity as we join in Christ's sacrifice; then we bring the gifts of bread and wine; and in the prayer over the gifts we ask the Lord to accept these gifts and make them the signs of his total self-giving. In this way we can introduce the Eucharistic Prayer without disturbance.

Is the washing of hands with the quiet prayer of the priest a remnant of the clerical liturgy? Is it more about the inner purity of the priest to make Christ's sacrifice? We can also ask: is the washing of hands with its symbolic meaning a repetition of the penitential act? Might it be better to move the penitential act to the beginning of the Liturgy of the Eucharist and, if we preserve the washing of hands, bring both rites together in a more expressive whole? Then

---

9. Cyril of Jerusalem, "Catecheses Mystagogicae Quinque," V, 2, *PG* 33, k. 1109–1110. English translation in Daniel J. Sheerin, *The Eucharist*, Message of the Fathers of the Church 7 (Wilmington: Delaware, 1986) 67–68.

10. In the previous numbering of the psalms this was Psalm 25.

we could preserve the *Kyrie* as an acclamation that is not supplanted by the penitential act. If we would also connect the rite of peace here, there would be a lot more clarity about the meaning behind these rituals—and clarity is the first requisite for active participation!

In connection with the symbolic meaning of the handwashing, the General Instruction apparently opposes the mere wetting of thumb and index finger over a miniscule dish and then drying them with a cloth that is even smaller than a handkerchief. In order to speak about an expressive rite—if one wants to keep the washing of hands—we might prefer to use a jug of water, a basin, and a towel with which the priest does indeed wash his hands.

The Prayer Over the Gifts

Orate fratres

Although the renewed eucharistic liturgy sees the *Orate fratres* as an invitation to the prayer that follows, we wonder whether it might not have been better to abolish it. Within the Consilium, the consultors of *coetus* 10 were advocates for abolishing it. Yet the bishops within the Consilium continued to demand its conservation, especially for pastoral reasons.

This invitation to pray is one of the oldest pre-Carolingian additions to the Roman eucharistic liturgy of Frankish origin. Originally, the celebrant addressed himself with these words to the priests surrounding him, who did not answer. Then the celebrant quietly said the prayer over the gifts (*secreta*) by which the Canon, said in a low voice, started. Later, at least in the time of Amalar of Metz (775–852), the priest also addressed the people.[11] In some medieval texts we even find the words "*fratres et sorores*," brothers and sisters. The call was in line with the idea that the priest was at the head of the people, and on behalf of the people he came before God. In this apology prayer, the priest asked the assembly to pray that he be worthy to bring the offering of all the people of God. The text of the invitation, included in the 1570 Roman Missal and kept in the 1970 Missal, comes from Italian sources in the twelfth century.

---

11. "Quo facto, revertitur ad populum sacerdos, et precatur ut orent pro illo, quatenus dignus sit universae plebis oblationem offerre domino," Amalarius, "De Ecclesiasticis Officiis Libri Quattor," Liber III, caput 19, *PL* 105, k. 1132.

Where originally neither the clerics nor the people gave an answer when asked for personal prayer, it gradually became the practice to answer with psalm verses, especially Psalm 19:15, and *suscipiat* settings. The formula used in the Tridentine Missal, maintained in the new Missal, also comes from Italy, where it was in practice since the eleventh century.

The liturgical movement understood this invitation and its response as an important element of active participation. There was so little in the clerical liturgy that involved the assembly that we can understand the consultors were looking for those few elements that were helpful to more active participation. One saw in this a confirmation of the participation of the faithful at the sacrifice: *meum ac vestrum sacrificium*. This was particularly helpful in the dialogued Masses. Yet in the *missa cantata* only the celebrant and his assistants said the *Orate fratres*. Hence, it is clear that several bishops within the Consilium and later at the Synod of Bishops in 1967 opposed any attempt to abolish this prayer. After all, something had grown around this formula. Other considerations besides pastoral ones played a part in this. Conservative bishops usually opposed the removal of any traditional elements. In addition, there was a certain conception about the sacrificial character of the Mass that was expressed in this formula.

In the clerical liturgy, the *Orate fratres* functioned as a sort of farewell to the celebrant by the faithful, whom he had asked to pray for him, before going alone into the silence (and the mysteriousness) of the Canon. In the renewed liturgy, the faithful are invited to follow and to participate in the eucharistic prayer that is said aloud in the vernacular and which has lost its mysteriousness. This is done through the introductory dialogue, the acclamation after the institution narrative, and the acclamation "Amen" at the concluding doxology.

Taking into account this remarkable difference, we may indeed ask whether the *Orate fratres* has lost its function. Before Vatican II, this invitation to pray was important for promoting active participation, but we can no longer say that today. Active participation is seen much more strongly by the participation of the faithful in the eucharistic prayer. In the final decision to keep the *Orate fratres*, the consultors were more concerned about not disrupting pious practices than about the logical and clear sequence of rites. This, however, had to be one of the guiding principles of the reform. Does the fact that in the renewed liturgy the faithful are explicitly invited to participate in the eucharistic prayer, and the preservation of the *Orate fratres* cause a repetition that should be avoided?

Another onerous factor for the preservation of the *Orate fratres* concerns the formula as such, more specifically the phrase *meum ac vestrum sacrificium*. Is this phrase a relic of the former clerical liturgy whereby the faithful had to be convinced that the sacrifice of the priest was also their sacrifice? Does the term *sacrificum* lead to a misunderstanding of the only sacrificial moment in the Eucharist that we mention previously? Indeed, we ask the Lord to accept the gifts in order to transform them into the actual signs of his sacrifice. The term *sacrificium*, however, suggests that it is *our* sacrifice. Are we stuck here in the concept of the offertory as a "little Canon"?

We can draw the conclusion here that preserving the *Orate fratres* is one of the clear indications of the compromised character of certain parts in the renewed liturgy.

The Prayer Over the Gifts

When the whole series of prayers and rites of the simplified offertory are finished, the expressive prayer of the entire rite occurs: the prayer over the gifts (*oratio super oblata*). In fact, this prayer, which resumes the main idea of the preparation of the gifts, would be sufficient once the gifts are brought and placed on the altar.

This prayer has regained its original name after being called *secreta* for centuries. It probably received the name *secreta*, or secret prayer, under Frankish influence where it was uttered in a low voice and led to the great silence during the Canon. Nevertheless, we find in some old sacramentaries the name *oratio super secreta*, the prayer over what is set aside (to be used for the Eucharist).[12] Already by the time of its first instruction, *Inter Oecumenici* (September 26, 1964), the Consilium had prescribed that the prayer be said in an audible voice so that the prayer would no longer be understood as a private prayer of the priest.[13]

---

12. From the Latin verb *secernere, secrevi, secretum* = to set apart, to separate, to isolate, to distinguish.

13. "*Instructio ad exsecutione constitutionis de sacra liturgia recte ordinandam*," *AAS* 56 (1964) 877–900 n 48 e.

The prayer over the gifts has the same function as the collect. As a presidential prayer, spoken in an audible voice and in the *orans* position, it concludes a particular part of the eucharistic celebration, that is, the preparation of the gifts. It should also be initiated by the invitation "Let us pray," which was originally the case. The prayer over the gifts does not only summarize the content and meaning of the preparation of the gifts, it also leads onward to the eucharistic prayer (cf. SC 77).

The terminology of the prayer expresses this. It speaks both about our gifts (*dona, munera, oblata*) and about their ultimate meaning when they have become the Body and Blood of Christ (*sacrificium, sancta*), so that some of the prayers give the impression that bread and wine are already the sacrifice.[14] Yet by this prayer, we present our gifts so that God would complete both them and us, who will be nourished by them, to become a living and pleasing offering. They are our gifts, but we already know their final destination, and we say this now proleptically. This is also the case with the prayer after communion, where we find the same terminology. There we speak about the gifts that have already been consumed. Here we speak about the gifts that will become the eucharistic gifts through the eucharistic prayer.

In the prayer over the gifts as an introduction to the eucharistic prayer, in contrast to the opening prayer, there is not always an allusion to the particular aspect of the celebration of the day. Actually, the attention is concentrated on the eucharistic event as such.

For active participation, it is important that the celebrant distinguish the importance of this prayer from the other parts of the preparation of the gifts, especially by the explicit way he pronounces the prayer and his use of the *orans* position. It is also very important that the faithful consciously agree to the prayer and make it the prayer of the community by their "Amen."

The Eucharistic Prayer

General Orientation

The General Instruction clearly says, "Now the center and high point of the entire celebration begins, namely, the Eucharistic Prayer

---

14. E.g., Tenth Sunday in Ordinary Time: "Look kindly upon our service, O Lord we pray, that what we offer may be an acceptable oblation to you and lead us to grow in charity."

itself, that is, the prayer of thanksgiving and sanctification" (78). Outside the new and surprising words of institution, Jesus joined the Jewish meal ritual, which appears in an expanded form at the Passover meal.[15] In this ritual, blessing, thanksgiving, memorial, and petition are central. These basic elements are therefore important to understand the Eucharist.

In the apostolic time the church continued to celebrate the Eucharist within the framework of a meal. Quite quickly, the rites around bread and wine were brought together under one eucharistic prayer. Around the middle of the second century, the rite was separated from the meal and preceded by a Liturgy of the Word. The eucharistic prayer was given greater individuality and expanded. There was no fixed text for this yet, however, and the presider personally formulated the eucharistic prayer, which had to remain recognizable to everyone in its basic elements. As Justin Martyr wrote, "The president then prays and gives thanks according to his ability." This free prayer speech continued until the fourth century, although we already find a written text for the eucharistic prayer in the beginning of the third century, the so-called Canon of Hippolytus. In addition to the basic elements of the eucharistic prayer, we also find here an institution narrative and an epiclesis.

In the East, different models of eucharistic prayers arose and continued to exist, usually divided according to two main types, the Alexandrian and the Antiochene. In the West, these came to a fixed formulation, the Roman Canon (canon = fixed rule; actually, *canon actionis* = the rule that determines the action), although other anaphora arose here as well, such as the Ambrosian-Milanese, the Spanish-Mozarabic, the Gallican, and the Celtic.

Already at the end of the fourth century the core of the prayers around the institution narrative, from the *Hanc igitur* to the *Supplices*, was fixed.[16] The final editing of the Roman Canon occurred

---

15. Although we are not sure that the Last Supper was in fact a Passover meal, Luke at least seems to connect it with the Passover meal as a memorial of the old covenant of which it is the fulfillment. In any case, as presider of a festal meal, Jesus could take advantage of the freedom to introduce adaptations to the traditional prayers and give them a new meaning.

16. Thus quoted in Ambrosius, *De sacramentis*, Liber IV, c. 5, 21–27. English translation in R.C.D. Jasper and G.J. Cuming, *Prayers of the Eucharist: Early and Reformed*, 3rd ed. (Collegeville, MN: Liturgical Press, 1987) 145–146.

under Pope Gregory the Great (590–604). Under the influence of Charlemagne (768–814), with his zeal for the restoration of the Roman Empire in Europe, the Roman liturgy, including the Roman Canon, gradually spread over the West. Since then the Roman church used, with a few minor exceptions, only this Canon.

Where originally the celebrant said the eucharistic prayer, as the presidential prayer par excellence, in an audible voice and in *orans* position, a remarkable change gradually took place. The priest began praying in silence, and more and more ritual gestures accompanied his prayer. When he mentioned the gifts, the priest also began to indicate them. This led to using the sign of the cross as a blessing gesture, as already mentioned in the eighth century. Since the eleventh century, the celebrant began to imitate Jesus' gestures at the Last Supper of taking bread and wine, eyes raised to heaven, blessing it, and so on while pronouncing the institution narrative. In the twelfth century, the practice of raising the host and the chalice for adoration by the people also arose. These and other practices, such as kneeling, bell ringing, and incensation, went together with an almost exclusive concentration on the institution narrative with the words of consecration.

The attention to the eucharistic prayer in its entirety of thanksgiving, praise, anamnesis, and supplication around bread and wine as the signs of the Lord, was lost this way. Eucharistic piety focused completely on the Real Presence (*praesentia realis*) of the Lord under the signs of bread and wine.[17] The theology became more and more involved in the problems of the Real Presence. Already in 825 AD, abbot Paschasius Radbertus and his monk Ratramnus had in Corbie a dispute about this Real Presence. In scholasticism, the question about the specific nature of the Real Presence resulted in the so-called transubstantiation doctrine, which the Council of Trent (1545–1563) preferred as a philosophical explanation. It was not until the twentieth century that theological reflection on the sacrament of the Eucharist could free itself from over emphasizing the Real Presence and the related question about the specific sacrificial character of the

17. Jozef Lamberts, "Liturgie et spiritualité de l'eucharistie au XIII⁵ siècle," ed. A. Haquin, *Fête-Dieu (1246–1996), 1. Actes du colloque de Liège, 12–14 septembre 1996*, Publications de l'Institut d'études médiévales 19/1 (Louvain-la-Neuve, 1999) 81–95.

celebration, by situating both elements in the broader context of the entire sacramental and ecclesial event of the Eucharist.

The silence during the Canon, related to the mysterious character of the consecration, was connected with splitting the original Canon into a preface and Canon, at least since the eighth century. In the oldest sacramentaries we find above the introduction of the preface: *incipit canon actionis,* while a document from the sixth century mentions that the people together with the priest sing the *Sanctus* "*infra actionem.*" The split originated in the Gallican liturgy when it was thought that the eucharistic prayer began with *Te igitur,* "we therefore," after the *Sanctus.* This became the Canon, and what preceded it was *praefatio,* or preface, interpreted as an introduction to the main prayer.

This word *praefatio* stood in the *Sacramentarium Hadrianum* above the *Vere dignum* texts, where, as the word *Canon,* it could refer to the entire eucharistic prayer. Here, the word *praefatio* could mean solemn, public proclamation or announcement. The Frankish liturgists found confirmation, therefore, in an indication in the *Ordo Romanus I.* This document says that after the *Sanctus* "the pontiff arises by himself and enters into the Canon" (*dum incipiunt dicere hymnum angelicum id est Sanctus; quem dum expleverint surgit pontifex solus et intrat in canone*).[18] This indication means that after the common singing of the *Sanctus* the presider alone continued to pronounce the Canon that had already begun with the introductory dialogue.

The separation between preface and Canon also became visible in the composition of the liturgical books. In the beginning of the eighth century, the *Te igitur* follows immediately after the *Sanctus* without any space between these prayers. A few years later, the T appears as an embellished initial. In the tenth century, the T was turned into a picture of the cross and in the twelfth century, this cross took a whole page and *Te igitur* began again with a capital T. In this way too the liturgical books made the separation visible.

With this separation, the church began to see the Canon more and more as a sanctuary that only the priest entered. A holy silence also

18. So, at least, in the longer version. In the short version: *surgit pontifex solus in canone.* Michel Andrieu, *Les Ordines Romani du haut Moyen Age,* part 2 (Leuven, 1948) 91 and 95.

belonged to this sanctuary, from which the people were excluded. In the *Ordo XV*, compiled in Frankish territory around the middle of the eighth century, it is said that the celebrant changes his tone, using a different voice so that he can be heard only by those standing at the altar (*dissimuli voci ita ut a circumadstantibus altare tantum audiantur*).[19] The *Ordo V*, a revision of the *Ordo Romanus I* from the middle of the ninth century, stipulates that only the celebrant is upright and begins the Canon in a low voice while the clergy around the altar remain bent in silence (*surgit pontifex solus et tacito intrat in canone*).[20]

The Missal of 1570 retained the separation of the preface and Canon and the silent saying of the Canon. This silence during the Canon was thus interpreted for centuries as a sacred silence, a dignified celebration of the miraculous coming of the Lord at the moment of the consecration and his sacred sacrifice.

Under the influence of liturgical-historical studies and the impulse of the liturgical movement, the conviction grew that the eucharistic prayer should not be denied to the faithful. The reforms of Vatican II led to seeing the eucharistic prayer again as a whole, praying it in an audible voice, and using the vernacular, like the other parts of the celebration.[21]

In its document *Eucharisticae participationem* of April 27, 1973, the Congregation for Divine Worship formulated its position about the demand for more eucharistic prayers.[22] At first, the number was limited to the four that are currently in the Roman Missal. The document also allowed, however, that the conferences of bishops could request permission to introduce new prayers to their territory for well-defined reasons and circumstances.[23] That is how the Dutch-speaking Belgian bishops received the approval of their own eucharistic prayer on April 9, 1976.

---

19. M. Andrieu, *o.c.* part 3, 103.

20. Ibid., part 2, 221.

21. "Instructio altera ad exsecutionem Constitutionis de Sacra Liturgia recte ordinandam," *AAS* 59 (1967) 442–448, n. 10 and 28.

22. "Litterae Circulares ad Conferentiarum Episcopalium Praesides de precibus eucharisticis," *Notitiae* 9 (1973) 193–201.

23. Ibid., n. 6.

On the occasion of the Holy Year 1975, the Congregation for Divine Worship issued two new eucharistic prayers for Masses of reconciliation. These anaphoras, provided with their own preface, were originally only to be used for a period of three years, but this period was subsequently extended several times "for other celebrations with the theme of reconciliation and penance, especially during Lent." Likewise, in 1975, three eucharistic prayers for Masses with children and young people were released. Eventually, ICEL made a translation of the so-called Swiss eucharistic prayer, approved for use in 1994. This prayer is officially titled Eucharistic Prayer for Masses for Various Needs and Occasions. It provides a choice of four prefaces with a corresponding set of intercessions, leading to four strands: The Church on the Way to Unity; God Guides the Church on the Way of Salvation; Jesus, Way to the Father; and Jesus, the Compassion of God. In all, there are thirteen eucharistic prayers approved by Rome for use in the United States at the present time.

Article 79 of the General Instruction briefly discusses the elements of the eucharistic prayer. First, however, we refer to article 78, which describes the meaning of the eucharistic prayer in this way:

> The Priest calls upon the people to lift up their hearts towards the Lord in prayer and thanksgiving; he associates the people with himself in the Prayer that he addresses in the name of the entire community to God the Father through Jesus Christ in the Holy Spirit. Furthermore, the meaning of this Prayer is that the whole congregation of the faithful joins with Christ in confessing the great deeds of God and in the offering of Sacrifice.

These words leave no doubt that the eucharistic prayer is an ecclesial prayer of thanksgiving and praise, of which the preface is an integral part and in which the whole community of faith must be involved.

The Thanksgiving or Preface

In its description of the Mass with a congregation, the General Instruction makes the preface again the solemn beginning of the church's great prayer of thanksgiving and praise. The word "preface" thus acquires more the meaning of a solemn proclamation in front of the people, who are then invited to agree, than a foreword that would precede the actual prayer of thanksgiving. The preface proclaims, in the presence of God, the expression of the proper tribute and gratitude of his people for the salvation that he gives.

The preface, or better the whole eucharistic prayer, starts with an introductory dialogue between the presider and the assembled people. This dialogue shows that we are not dealing here with an ordinary presidential prayer, which begins with the invitation to pray together, but with the presidential prayer par excellence.[24] In this dialogue, gratitude is already central: "Let us give thanks to the Lord, our God." / "It is right to give him thanks and praise."

This dialogue between presider and people is a very old liturgical datum, which we find in all liturgies, and it probably goes back to the time of the apostles. It can be found in the Canon of Hippolytus. In the texts of Augustine, we find this dialogue several times, for example, in his *Sermo 227* where he discusses the *Sursum corda* as follows:

> So, at the words "Lift up your hearts," you respond, "We have lifted them up to the Lord." And, lest you attribute your having your hearts to the Lord on high to your own strength, your own merits, your own efforts, since it is God's gift to have one's heart lifted up, for this reason the bishop or the priest who is offering the sacrifice, immediately after the people have replied "We have lifted our hearts up to the Lord," continues "Let us give thanks to the Lord our God," that we have our hearts lifted up. Let us give thanks, for, were it not for His gift, we would have our hearts on earth. And you bear witness, saying "It is fitting and right" that we give thanks to Him who has caused us to raise up our hearts to our Head.[25]

We already find a similar acclamation as "it is right and just" (*dignum et justum est*) in the Jewish morning prayer. In the Hellenistic culture too, the people's assembly expressed its consent to an important decision by means of these or similar formulas. Therefore,

---

24. Refer to what has been said about the *Orate fratres* as introduction to the prayer over the gifts.

25. Augustinus, "Sermo 227. In die Paschae IV. Ad infantes, de sacramentis," *PL* 38, k 1100. English translation in Jasper and Cuming, *Prayers of the Eucharist*, *o.c.*, 97–98.

when this formula begins to function in the liturgy within that cultural context, this means that the assembled faith community gives its assenting participation when the priest, as presider, starts the church's prayer of thanksgiving. Thus, the eucharistic prayer also appears to be an ecclesial prayer, in which the hierarchical structure of the church is expressed. The priest says the thanksgiving prayer on behalf of the assembled people he presides over. That is how John Chrysostom could already testify: "Not only the priest performs the thanksgiving, but the people with him."[26]

In order to promote active participation, once again it will be necessary to explain in our liturgical catechesis the meaning of the preface that the priest, on behalf of the congregation that he invites to join his prayer, addresses to the Father as homage and thanksgiving of the church, through and with Christ in the unity of the Spirit. It will also be necessary to draw attention to the central motive of each preface, namely, the work of salvation that God does for us especially through Christ.

The Acclamation of the Sanctus

Originally, the *Sanctus* was an acclamation song of the whole people. However, especially in the West, it gradually became a polyphonic chant of the choir. The priest prayed it for himself and continued with *Te igitur* while the choir was singing. The *Sanctus* is now restored as an acclamation by the people and became one of the important elements of active participation (GIRM 79b). This way the people can jubilantly join in the prayer of thanksgiving that the priest says on behalf of all.

Its content makes it evident that the *Sanctus*, which is composed of two biblical quotations, Isaiah 6:3 and Matthew 21:9, has a clear acclamation character. The faithful community joins in the song of praise to God, who has shown his glory to heaven and earth. This glory, or *kabod*, of God has especially shown itself in the person of Jesus. In him, God has shown himself as a God who cares for people, a God who helps people recognize their rights. Therefore, the three-time repetition of "holy" (*Trisagion*) turns into the jubilant welcome

---

26. Joannes Chrysostomos, "In Secundam ad Corinthios Epistolam commentarium," *PG* 61, k 527.

of "he who comes in the name of the Lord," in whom the glory, *kabod,* or *doxa* of God has fully appeared among us.

The original meaning of *Hosanna,* "save us, come to our aid" (Ps 118:25), had already in the synagogue liturgy been transformed into praise for the one who helps. The *Sanctus* refers to Matthew 21:9, where on Jesus' entry into Jerusalem the people cry out, "Hosanna to the Son of David! Blessed is he who comes in the name of the Lord! Hosanna in the highest!" In this way we welcome the presence of Christ in the eucharistic gifts.

The Epiclesis

As derived from the Greek *epikaleoo,* "epiclesis" means to call down, to invoke, to invite. As used in liturgy, the word means that we invoke God, specifically the Holy Spirit, to sanctify a person or a thing.[27] In this sense, we may already say that the entire eucharistic prayer is an invocation of God's name over the gifts and over the congregation. More than once this has been forgotten in the Western eucharistic theology with its overemphasis on the words of institution. The priest, by virtue of his ordination, could realize almost arbitrarily the consecration, the changing of bread and wine into the Body and Blood of Christ. When the presider pronounces the eucharistic prayer, however, he acts as a faithful and obedient servant of the Lord according to the mandate to do what Jesus did during the Last Supper. That is why, as the one who presides over the congregation, he must invoke God for the completion of the gifts that are brought forward by the congregation gathered together to celebrate the memorial.

This invocation actually appeared in the previous Roman Canon through the divine titles, such as Lord, Holy Father, almighty and eternal God. It happened when, in the *Quam oblationem,* the priest asked God "to make this offering wholly blessed, approved, ratified, reasonable, and acceptable; that it may become to us the body and blood of your dearly beloved Son Jesus Christ our Lord," as well as in the *Supplices,* where the priest asked God, "that all of us who have

---

27. Jozef Lamberts, "May Your Holy Spirit, Lord Come . . . Some Reflections on the Epiclesis," *Ephrem's Theological Journal* 2 (1998) 99–115.

received the most holy body and blood of your Son by partaking at this altar may be filled with all heavenly blessing and grace."

When these prayers expressly call the Holy Spirit as the performer of God's grace, then we can speak about an epiclesis in the strictest sense. Although the invocations noted above do not mention the Holy Spirit, we may nevertheless call them an epiclesis in a more general sense.

In the new eucharistic prayers, we find this epiclesis explicitly at two locations: before the institution narrative and after the anamnesis. This does justice to a development in the Catholic theology of the last decades that rediscovered the Holy Spirit, who completes the work of salvation toward the end times. We can only applaud that a step was taken in the direction of the Eastern Rite churches, which, through their observers at the Council, expressed their surprise at the fact that the Holy Spirit occupied such a poor place in the theology and liturgy of the Roman church.[28]

Already in the oldest authentic eucharistic prayer, that of the *Traditio Apostolica* generally attributed to Hippolytus of Rome and dated about 215, we find an explicit epiclesis placed after the institution narrative. This epiclesis is not a consecration epiclesis, but rather a communion epiclesis since it asks that those partaking in the offering be gathered together into one, and that they be filled with the Holy Spirit for the strengthening of their faith so that they might praise God. The text is as follows:

> And we ask that you would send your Holy Spirit upon the offering of your holy Church; that, gathering her into one, you would grant to all who receive the holy things (to receive) for the fullness of the Holy Spirit for the strengthening of faith in truth; that we may praise and glorify you through your child Jesus Christ . . . [29]

This epiclesis does not speak about the transformation of the gifts. The first evident witness of a consecration epiclesis is to be

---

28. Yves Congar demonstrated that this remark is a little exaggerated. Yves Congar, "Pneumatologie ou 'Christomonisme' dans la tradition latine?," *Ecclesia a Spiritu Sancto edocta* (*Mélanges théologiques Mgr. G. Philips*) (Gembloux, 1970) 41–63.

29. English translation from Jasper and Cuming, *Prayers of the Eucharist*, 35.

found in the *Mystagogical Catecheses* of bishop Cyril of Jerusalem (died 386). Already in the first of these five lectures for the newly baptized he explains:

> The bread and wine of the Eucharist before the holy invocation (*epiklèsioos*) of the Adorable Trinity was simply bread and wine. While after the invocation the bread becomes the body of Christ and the wine the blood of Christ (1,7,5).[30]

A polemic about the consecration epiclesis arose between the East and West. In the heat of the conflict, the Roman Rite churches held the belief that the words of institution were when transubstantiation occurred, while the Eastern Rite churches were of the opinion that the epiclesis was the moment when the bread and wine was changed into the Body and Blood of Christ. Both sides forgot that the whole eucharistic prayer, besides being a prayer of praise and thanksgiving, is a supplication to God to complete and accept our gifts as Body and Blood and to transform us, who participate in them, into Christ's ecclesial Body on earth.

Eventually the struggle ended and the eucharistic prayer was recognized as a unit. Yet the Roman Canon did not mention the Holy Spirit anywhere, neither in the prayer of conversion of the gifts nor in the prayer of transformation of the faithful community. In the new eucharistic prayers we find an explicit mention of the Spirit both in the consecration epiclesis and in the communion epiclesis.

The elaboration of the communion epiclesis in the new eucharistic prayers is germane for the active participation of the faithful. It explicitly asks that the Holy Spirit determine the lives of those who have gathered around bread and cup. This makes it clear to the faithful that the consecration is not an end in itself, merely recognizing the presence of Christ under the species of bread and wine. The consecration or presence of the Lord is oriented toward communion, our partaking of him who suffered, died, was resurrected, and ascended into heaven to live with the Father. From there he

---

30. Translated from *Cyril von Jerusalem. Mystagogicae Catecheses Mystagogischen Katechesen. Griechisch-Deutsch. Übersetzt und eingeleilet von Georg Rowekamp*. Fontes Christiani 7 (Freiburg-Basel-Wien . . . , 1992) 102–105.

continues to work through his Spirit, who now drives us to grow in love and unity to become the church, the Body of Christ on earth. Therefore, it is fitting that we pray after the consecration, as in Canon III: "[G]rant that we, who are nourished by the Body and Blood of your Son and filled with his Holy Spirit, may become one body, one spirit in Christ."

In this way it is possible that the celebrating community becomes aware that they are also the subject of the eucharistic celebration, that when they come together to do what the Lord did, they are actually placed in an analogous situation to Jesus. To be able to do this, the assembled community asks for the Spirit, who unites and completes. The revaluation of the epiclesis is more than a step toward unity with the Eastern Rite churches. It is above all an important element for a conscious participation in the eucharistic celebration.

Institution Narrative and Consecration

We have pointed out already that the institution narrative, which is the core of the eucharistic prayer, should not be isolated from the whole of it. Nor can the eucharistic prayer be isolated from the communion rite. The name "institution narrative" should not make us forget that it is a prayer and not a report about a certain event from antiquity. The founding event of every eucharistic celebration is present here in prayer, in the sense of the Jewish memorial.

The Western emphasis on the institution narrative, especially with the words of institution as a consecration formula, has caused much difficulty in a correct understanding of the institution narrative as a prayer. In the Roman Canon, God was explicitly addressed in the institution narrative: "to you, O God, his almighty Father, giving you thanks . . . and once more giving you thanks." Yet no attention was paid to this and it almost became a magical pronouncing of the words: "*Hoc est enim corpus meum—Hic est enim calix sanguinis mei, novi et aeterni testamenti, mysterium fidei, qui pro vobis et pro multis effundetur in remissionem peccatorum.*" These words were printed in uppercase letters in each Missal. By speaking these words, the miracle could happen: bread and wine became the Body and Blood of Christ.

The texts of the institution narrative that were handed down from the oldest traditions were different from each other, and different from the biblical texts. After all, the liturgy was already being celebrated before Paul and the evangelists began their writings. This helps to explain why they differ from each other. Characteristic for the texts in the Roman Canon is an attempt to include as many biblical elements as possible in them, a clear parallelism between the words over the bread and cup, as well as a number of extensions to enrich the text theologically and spiritually. The most enigmatic of these additions is the expression "*mysterium fidei.*"

The Synod of Bishops, who in 1967 approved the introduction of the new anaphoras, also accepted the proposal to simplify the consecration words over the bread to "This is my Body which will be given up for you" and to omit *mysterium fidei* from the words prayed over the cup. The new Missal made the words of institution the same for each of the four eucharistic prayers, and later, also for the other anaphoras. The priest introducing the memorial acclamation transforms it into a dialogue by saying, "The mystery of faith," to which the congregation responds in one of three ways. The words spoken by the priest are no longer, "Let us proclaim the mystery of faith," and the third edition of the Roman Missal refers to the memorial acclamation as "The mystery of faith."

The Anamnesis

The concluding words of the institution narrative evoke the anamnesis or memorial: "Do this in memory of me." The whole eucharistic prayer, even the whole eucharistic celebration, is to keep doing what the Lord has asked us to do to remember him. That is why, because the whole eucharistic prayer is thanksgiving and praise, not only the preface, the whole eucharistic prayer is also anamnetic. In the liturgy we keep the term "anamnesis" for the prayer that begins with the words, "Therefore, O Lord, as we celebrate the memorial . . ." and what follows: his passion, death, resurrection, ascension, and in some of the settings, his second coming.[31] The latter is not part of the anamnesis as such, but is clearly in the perspective of the anamnesis: in the risen and glorified Lord we have the promise of his second coming.

---

31. This is the case in the Eucharistic Liturgy of the Apostolic Constitutions of Basil and of James. In the third and fourth canons of the new Roman Missal and in the first canon for reconciliation we pray that the anamnesis happens, looking forward to his second coming.

Together with prayers of praise, thanksgiving, and supplication, the anamnesis is one of the original elements of the eucharistic prayer, going back to its design in the Jewish *berakah*, where praise and thanksgiving led to remembering God's acts of salvation. The rich diversity of anamnetic elements in the many prefaces of the revised Missal provides us a true creed that, in terms of size and lyrical elaboration, far surpasses the dogmatically formulated Nicene-Constantinopolitan Creed. The fourth eucharistic prayer in particular depicts a rich fresco of salvation history. The anamnesis explicitly thematizes this memorial of Christ's paschal mystery, which consists of his suffering, death, resurrection, and ascension. It is because of this that we celebrate the Eucharist: to remember the Lord in these decisive events.

A more recent form of anamnesis, preceding the presidential anamnesis, is the acclamation by the faithful immediately after the institution narrative. Such acclamations already existed in the East-ern Rite anaphora, for example, with the Copts.[32] We have here a remarkable expression of active participation precisely in the center of the eucharistic prayer. While in the three other acclamations dur-ing the eucharistic prayer the faithful agree with the priest's prayer, they now anticipate what the priest will develop in his presidential anamnesis. The whole community takes over, as it were, leading the anamnetic confession of the eucharistic event, to which the priest as presider joins. This confirms that the subject of the anamnesis, as of the whole eucharistic celebration, is not the priest, but the people of God. Here justice is done to the baptismal priesthood of the faithful, which empowers them to celebrate the Eucharist.

This explicit confirmation of the faithful community as subject of the anamnesis should not make us forget that the anamnesis in the Roman Canon also started with the words " *Unde et memores, Domini, nos servi tui, sed et plebs tua sancta . . . ,*" "wherefore, Lord, we your servants, but also your holy people, mindful . . ." This confirmation, however, received little or no attention because all focus was on the consecration as the true coming of the Lord, but

---

32. "We proclaim your death, we confess your resurrection, and we pray" (The Deir Balizeh Papyrus). "Your death, Lord, we proclaim and your resurrection we confess" (The Liturgy of St. James).

also because this anamnesis was pronounced in a whisper and in a completely foreign language.

Both the anamnetic acclamation and the presidential anamnesis differ from the rest of the eucharistic prayer, in that they are addressed to Christ, where the priest directs the eucharistic prayer to the Father. It is characteristic of the Roman liturgy that hymns and acclamations were addressed to Christ as spontaneous expressions of popular piety. This is the case with the *Kyrie*, the second part of the Gloria, and the *Agnus Dei*. The *Benedictus* of the *Sanctus* also addresses Christ and functioned not so long ago as a confession of the Real Presence of Christ after the consecration.

The Order of Mass provides three anamnetic acclamations, from which one can freely choose. The first acclamation "We proclaim your Death, O Lord, and profess your Resurrection until you come again" seems to be the most meaningful. It corresponds to 1 Corinthians 11:26, explicitly mentions the paschal mystery, holds the Parousia, expresses the proclamation character of Jesus' command to celebrate the Eucharist in memory of him, and is the most traditional. The second acclamation is an almost literal representation of 1 Corinthians 11:26: "When we eat this Bread and drink this Cup, we proclaim your Death, O Lord, until you come again." This acclamation has a disadvantage in that it does not explicitly mention the resurrection. The third acclamation is "Save us, Savior of the world, for by your Cross and Resurrection you have set us free." Here the passion and the resurrection are mentioned, but the tenor of this text is more that of a prayer (*prex*) than of an acclamation.[33]

The Offering (Oblation)

The oblation is strongly connected with the anamnesis. To celebrate the Eucharist is, after all, not only a memorial of Jesus' paschal mystery as a historical fact, but also an offering to the Father in the present moment. This essential link between anamnesis and oblation is expressed in the fact that both blend into one prayer text. This is especially apparent in the Latin formulation of the Roman Canon:

---

33. The fourth response that was used in the US, "Christ has died, Christ is risen, Christ will come again," is no longer approved since it simply states what Christ has done instead of addresses Christ.

"*unde et memores . . . offerimus,*" translated as "Wherefore we . . . mindful . . . offer." The eucharistic prayers of the new Missal formulates it this way: "Therefore, as we celebrate the memorial of . . . we offer you . . . " This refers us to "anaphora," the other name for the eucharistic payer, which was the favored name in the first centuries of Christianity. The word is derived from the Greek *anapheroo* that means "to offer." In this sense, we can look at the eucharistic prayer as a whole, which we have already been able to characterize as a prayer of praise and thanksgiving, and as anamnesis, and see one large offering prayer. The oblation explicitly thematizes this aspect.

Especially as a reaction against the Protestant refusal to accept the Eucharist as "sacrifice of the church," this aspect led sometimes to an overemphasis on the offering character of the eucharistic prayer. It is therefore important to clarify that in the anamnesis, the faith community commemorates the paschal mystery of Christ. In highest thankfulness, we put this gift, Christ's Body and Blood under the species of bread and wine, back in front of the giver, God, and present it to him through the oblation. Through his paschal mystery, Christ also offers his church to the Father. Through our baptism, we participate in Christ's paschal mystery and we became his church. This way, by virtue of our baptism, together with and in Christ, we can give ourselves to the Father as a pleasing offering.

We will only be able to do this, however, as far as we also try to live like Christ. This is precisely why we ask in the communion epiclesis that we who are going to celebrate our union with Christ through communion may also be filled with his Spirit. It is the same divine Spirit, who worked in Jesus and incited him to a total engagement with the needs of the people, who must animate us for an effective engagement. Only through our actual commitment to others, which the Spirit encourages and strengthens us for, can we offer ourselves as church together with Christ to the Father. Only then will the oblation or offertory obtain its full meaning, as within the eucharistic prayer the anamnesis, the oblation, and the epiclesis form a whole.

Intercessions

Already in the Jewish *berakah*, the praise, thanksgiving, and anamnesis emerged into the supplication (*tephillah*): "Have mercy, Lord our God, on Israel your people, on Jerusalem your city, on your sanctuary and your dwelling. . . ." Our supplication begins in the epiclesis, especially when we ask that the Spirit complete the work of salvation in and by us. This supplication continues in the intercessions. We find these prayers in the very oldest liturgies, and also in the *Traditio Apostolica* of Hippolytus. At first glance, they may seem to be a repetition of the prayer of the faithful, or universal prayer. The very fact that they existed in the oldest liturgies, however, prove that they are not a repetition.

We have already pointed out the difference between these two prayers. The intercessions aim at the unity of the church as far as it is the fruit of the Eucharist. Around the celebration of Christ's paschal mystery, this unity is experienced both with the whole earthly church and with the heavenly church. Especially with regard to the earthly church, the mention of the pope and bishop expresses the ecclesial dimension of every eucharistic celebration. The assembled faith community can only celebrate the Eucharist because the presider, by virtue of his ordination that allows him to participate in the priesthood of the bishop in connection with the world episcopate, represents the church in its hierarchical structure *hic et nunc.*

The Final Doxology

The eucharistic prayer concludes with the solemn praise of God's glory, the final doxology. The faith community, gathered to celebrate Christ's paschal mystery in thanksgiving and brought together in unity through the Holy Spirit, now expresses its complete praise for the Father. This doxology is not a wish that God may be glorified, but the effective glorification of God by the gathered people of God.

The biblical meaning of God's glory, expressed through the Hebrew word *kabod*, points to the impressive way in which God shows his being, namely, as a God who cares for us without restriction. God has fully showed this *kabod* in Jesus Christ, who indeed committed himself to the salvation of the people without restriction until death. God's *kabod* is now also revealed on earth when we, remembering Jesus' total self-giving and celebrating our union with him through communion, stimulated by the Spirit, commit ourselves to others. Only then will God's name be fully praised.

When the priest as presider says or sings the final doxology, he takes the chalice and the paten with the host, Christ's Body and

Blood, and lifts them up in a gesture of offering. This gesture clearly underscores the importance of the doxology: it is through Christ's life, passion, death, and resurrection that God's glory has fully manifested itself.

We are dealing here with an extremely important element of active participation when the faithful answer this solemn doxology with their "Amen." Our liturgical catechesis cannot point enough to the consequences this "Amen" of the celebrating community implies. As a community, united with Christ and under the impetus of his Spirit, we are committed to establish God's glory on earth. Seen in this way, to celebrate the Eucharist is not a free matter. To participate actively challenges our whole being. Understood in its extreme consequence, our celebration of the Eucharist becomes a "dangerous anamnesis." The memory of Jesus' suffering, death, and resurrection, through which God has revealed his glory, places us in solidarity with the suffering and the weak. It calls us to a full commitment to the coming of God's kingdom.

Common Pronouncing of the Eucharistic Prayer?

There is a desire in some parishes for the priest and the faithful to say the eucharistic prayer together, alternating it in a division of roles or assigning some texts to the faithful. Yet this is a misunderstanding of active participation and a misconception of the genre of this prayer.

First, in our eucharistic prayer we must be able to recognize what Christ did during the Last Supper. The basic structure of Christ's thanksgiving at the Last Supper is the Jewish *berakah*, or blessing. The father of the house alone pronounced the *berakah* after having asked for the consent of his table companions, and the acclamation of all concluded the *berakah*. In this same manner, the Christian tradition reserved the eucharist prayer for the priest who speaks *in persona Christi Capitis.*

Second, this prayer is certainly not a private prayer, even when said only by the priest. The presider says the prayer in the name of the whole assembly, the Spirit-inspired ecclesial Body of Christ, in which the Spirit enables him as ministerial priest to act *in persona Christi Capitis*. In this sense the priest also speaks *in persona ecclesiae*, because by the charism of his ordination he is authorized to represent Christ as the head within this concrete manifestation and experience of Christ's body, the church. Although the priest does not need to be authorized by the congregation, the congregation needs to agree and understand their union with their presider in order to give the eucharistic prayer its full ecclesial dimension. In this way, the eucharistic prayer becomes the prayer of the gathered people of God, incorporated in Christ and inspired by the Spirit, by which they express to the Father their perfect praise and thanksgiving and bring to him the sacrifice.

The faithful explicitly express their involvement and consent through the introductory dialogue, the *Sanctus*, the anamnetic acclamation, and the Amen after the final doxology. They do this equally through their attentive willingness to listen. To claim that the faithful need to constantly do and speak in the liturgy would be a danger to true active participation. Such a form of participation could lead to formalism, a liturgy where everyone is busy but without an inner experience.

If one wants to let the faithful speak more during the eucharistic prayer, without neglecting the inherent genre of this prayer, without denying the liturgical function of priest and faithful, one could think to introduce a greater number of acclamations. The introduction of the anamnetic acclamation was a first step. It should be noted too that the eucharistic prayers for Masses with Children already have more acclamations.

Our approach to an ecclesial liturgy has shown that saying the eucharistic prayer by the priest alone does not mean a clerical setting apart, on the contrary. It is not a question of reserving and excluding, or even providing something more for the priest. It would be sad if rancorous feelings should play a role in demanding a greater contribution of the lay faithful in the eucharistic prayer.

The Communion Rite

General Orientation

The communion rite should be in line with the eucharistic prayer, and we must test the renewed rite on this principle. If there is a need to work on the clarity of the renewed rite, as the Constitution on the Liturgy requested in article 50, it is especially here where the faithful are invited to fully participate in the celebration by receiving communion. This act is indeed the culmination of the entire eucharistic celebration and the high point of active participation of the faithful.

How are these principles taken into account in the renewed communion rite? Has active participation of the faithful been promoted in the communion rite? Have we said farewell to certain excesses that, over the course of history, have obscured the actual rite? Or have they been retained, somewhat modified, in the opinion that one had to remain faithful to tradition?

In the Tridentine Missal, there was no mention of the faithful receiving communion. As far as they wanted to receive communion it was necessary to introduce into the Mass the ritual for distributing communion to the sick. This rite consisted of the *Confiteor*, followed by the *Missereatur* and absolution, to which were added the *Ecce Agnus Dei*, which the priest said while showing the host to the communicants, and the threefold *Domine, non sum dignus*, which the faithful said in response. Communion could be given before, during, or after Mass and by someone other than the celebrating priest. Under the pressure of the liturgical movement, the communion of the faithful began to take place more and more immediately after the communion of the celebrant. However, the ritual for communion of the sick was still used for the communion of the faithful.

In the renewed liturgy, communion of the congregation is not only clearly integrated in the rite, but the faithful are also constantly involved in the event. The preparation for communion forms a series of ordered unities: the Lord's Prayer, the sign of peace, and the fraction rite. Nevertheless, we will have to formulate some critical remarks regarding the current practice.

The Lord's Prayer

The Invitation
Before the faith community prays the Our Father together, the priest invites the assembly to do so. The former *Oremus*, or "Let us pray," has been omitted, and this is justified. Why should the priest, after the prayer par excellence, in which the entire community has joined by acclamation, still invite the faithful to pray? The new Roman Missal has kept the formulation of the former missal, but with new language: "At the Savior's command and formed by divine teaching, we dare to say." By omitting the *Oremus* this formulation is functional here.

This formulation has a very old origin and is more or less identical to a comment of Cyprian (died 258) on the Our Father:

> Among the saving commandments (*praecepta*) and divine teaching (*monita*) that the Lord has left us for the salvation of his people, he has included a formula of prayer; he himself has taught us what we should ask for.[34]

This text does not prove that the Lord's Prayer with the invitation would have been used in the eucharistic celebration at the time of Cyprian. The context of this text has no reference to the Eucharist. It refers, rather, to the use of the Our Father in praying during the day. It is certain, however, that in the days of Pope Gregory the Great (590–604), the Lord's Prayer with the admonition appeared at the same place in the eucharistic celebration.

Although the 1970 Roman Missal provided only one invitation, the *Litterae Circulares* of April 27, 1973 already said that other formulations could be used. This document asked, however, to avoid any verbosity.[35] The Order of Mass in English provides four formulations. In line with the freedom that the *Litterae Circulares* provides and from a pastoral sense, the presider can find a formulation that fits the congregation or the special aspect of the celebration, and which allows for more active participation.

The Lord's Prayer

In the years immediately after Vatican II, there was a lot of discussion about the place of the Lord's Prayer in the eucharistic celebration. Some councilors wanted to remove it from the Liturgy of the Eucharist. Their argument was that in the oldest sources, the

---

34. Cyprianus, "De oratione dominica 2," *PL* 4, k 520.

35. "Naturally these admonitions need not be given word for word as set out in the Missal, so much so that it may well be advisable, at least in certain instances, to adapt them somewhat to the actual circumstances of the particular gathering. Nevertheless, in giving these admonitions their particular character is to be preserved, so that they do not turn into sermons or homilies; and care must be taken to be brief, and verbosity, wearisome to the participants, must be avoided." "Eucharistiae participationem," 14, *Notitiae* 9 (1973) 193–201, 199.

Apologia of Justin and the *Traditio Apostolica* of Hippolytus, there was no indication of the Our Father in the eucharistic celebration. Nor was this the case in the *Constitutiones Apostolorum* and the *Euchologion of Serapion*, although there was already a tendency to have communion preceded by an introductory prayer.

Relying on the principle that the renewed Liturgy of the Eucharist must be more transparent and more closely connected with the event during the Last Supper, one might at first glance justify the omission of the Lord's Prayer from the communion rite. If one does not want to go so far, one could place it at the end of the Liturgy of the Word or in the concluding rite, as in other sacramental celebrations outside the Eucharist.

On the other hand, the inclusion of the Lord's Prayer in the communion rite began to take effect from the end of the fourth century, and from then gradually became scattered in all liturgies. In asking for our daily bread, the church fathers saw a connection with Christ's eucharistic presence under the species of bread. This largely influenced, if not caused, the inclusion of the Lord's Prayer in the communion rite.

In a text of Ambrose of Milan (ca. 340–397) the Lord's Prayer appears already to be included in the communion rite, although it cannot be determined whether before or after the fraction rite.[36] Augustine says in one of his sermons to the new baptized:

> After the sanctification of the divine sacrifice has been effected, we say the Lord's Prayer, the prayer which you were taught and have recited.[37]

Concerning the place of the Lord's Prayer within the communion rite, different developments occurred within the different liturgies. The Roman, Byzantine, Armenian, and Maronite liturgies placed the Lord's Prayer before the fraction rite, immediately after the eucharistic prayer, while all the other rites, not only the non-Byzantine

---

36. Ambrosius, "De Sacramentis, Liber V," c. 6,24, *PL* 16, k 452.

37. Augustinus, "Sermo 227. Ad infantes, de Sacramentis," *PL* 38, k 1101. Augustine alludes to the "*traditio*" and the following "*redditio*" of the Lord's Prayer during the preparation for baptism.

Eastern Rites but also the other Western Rites, placed it after the fraction rite.

It was Pope Gregory the Great (590–604) who placed the Lord's Prayer in the Roman liturgy right after the eucharistic prayer, and thus before the fraction rite. We can deduce his motivation for doing this from the reply he wrote to Bishop John of Syracuse (Sicily), who accused Gregory of taking over Greek customs in the Roman liturgy:

> Here is why we say the Lord's Prayer right after the Canon. The custom of the apostles was to consecrate the sacrifice solely by means of the prayer of offering. It seemed to me quite inappropriate, on the one hand, to say over the offering a prayer composed by one or other writer and, on the other, not to say over the redeemer's body and blood the prayer which he himself composed and which tradition has preserved for us. But, whereas among the Greeks the prayer is said by the entire congregation, among us the priest alone says it.[38]

Gregory apparently took offense that bread and wine were consecrated by a mere human prayer and not by the prayer that the Lord himself taught us. In fact, he intended to give the Lord's Prayer, which until then only functioned as a preparatory prayer, a consecratory dimension by letting it follow right after the Canon and before the fraction rite. But Pope Gregory mistakenly referred to an apostolic tradition. Apart from his motivation, this can be explained from the practice at that time of the Pontifical Mass. After the eucharistic prayer was said at the altar by the pope, he returned to his *cathedra*, or chair, while the concelebrants took their places again in the apse. The deacons then brought the eucharistic bread for the fraction rite. Then one prayed the Lord's Prayer as immediate preparation for communion (the *Agnus Dei* was not yet sung then). Pope Gregory repositioned the fraction rite and the Lord's Prayer so that this prayer could be said at the altar.

Once the Lord's Prayer followed immediately after the eucharistic prayer, the way was paved to make this pre-eminently communal

---

38. Gregorius Magnus, "Epistula XII ad Ioanem episcopum Syracusanum," *PL* 77, k 956–957.

prayer into a presidential prayer. This happened in the Roman liturgy, while in the East the Lord's Prayer continued to belong to the community. In the West, the faithful could only join the Lord's Prayer by saying the final petition. Apparently, it had been forgotten that the older introductory formula that stated, "*We* dare to say" could only refer to the whole community.

The first Instruction on the Implementation of the Constitution on the Sacred Liturgy of 1964 restored the Lord's Prayer as communal prayer during the eucharistic celebration, encouraging all the faithful to say or sing it.[39] This decision enabled the prayer to become a full element of active participation.

Deviating from the oldest liturgies, the councilors opted to keep the Lord's Prayer in the place it had in the Roman liturgy since Pope Gregory the Great. Without following Gregory's motivation, several commentators interpreted the function of the Lord's Prayer as a kind of hinge prayer, one with a bridge function. Its first part links in substance with the eucharistic prayer, of which it is somewhat a summary. The second part is then a special preparation for communion.

The Embolism and the Doxological Acclamation

As the Lord's Prayer appears to be meaningful in this place, it is not so clear for the subsequent embolism (insertion). In comparison with the past, this prayer is markedly shorter by the omission of the series of saints' names and now ends with an eschatological sound, to which people can connect with a doxological acclamation.

Within the *coetus* that prepared the new Order of Mass some proposed omitting the embolism because it does not add anything essential to the Lord's Prayer and is only an elaboration of the last petition. Moreover, in its petition for peace it repeats the subsequent rite of peace. Such doubling had to be avoided according to the principles of the Constitution on the Liturgy. We could also say that this embolism, although shorter, means an unnecessary complication in

---

39. "Inter Oecumenici," n. 48, *AAS* 56 (1964) 887–900, 888. This put an end to the confused situation since the Instruction of September 3, 1958, because this way the Lord's Prayer kept its presidential character in the sung Masses, whereas in the read Masses it functioned as a prayer of the community. Cf. *AAS* 50 (1958) 630–663, 643 n. 32.

the transition from the eucharistic prayer to communion, which for the sake of clarity had to be as short as possible.

We find the embolism in all Western and Eastern liturgies, however, except for the Byzantine. The Gallican liturgy even had varied formulations. This is what Alphonse Raes, SJ, an expert in Eastern liturgies, underscored.[40] When consulted on this, he insisted strongly on the preservation of the embolism and saw in it an element of ecumenical understanding. The Consilium considered this and opted to preserve the embolism, albeit with the aforementioned adjustment.

We can explain the omission of the intercession of the saints, by which the embolism became shorter, by noting that this does not occur in the Eastern and Gallican liturgies. Also, it can be seen as a repetition of the intercessions in the Roman Canon. The shorter embolism has an eschatological perspective, adopted from Titus 2:13. This eschatological dimension is contained already in the Lord's Prayer, and is typical for our eucharistic celebration in the expectation of the ultimate supper with the Lord, when we will experience total liberation and complete shalom.

This eschatological end leads easily to the people's doxological acclamation: "For the kingdom, the power, and the glory are yours, now and for ever." This doxology derives from the oldest liturgies and appears in some manuscripts of the Gospel of Matthew (Matt 6:13). It was handed down in the *Didache* at the end of the first century as the conclusion of the Lord's Prayer.[41] Almost all Eastern liturgies adopted this doxology. The churches of the Reformation, except the Lutheran churches in Scandinavia, conclude the Lord's Prayer with this doxology. The adoption in the Roman eucharistic liturgy is a recognition of a very old tradition, and an ecumenical gesture as well.

It remains a question whether the embolism between the Lord's Prayer and the doxology was necessary. Would it not have been better to end the Our Father with the doxology? Was the oldest practice, whereby the Lord's Prayer was said after the fraction rite as immediate preparation for communion, more meaningful? Would

40. The well-known standard work of this author: Alphonse Raes, *Introductio in liturgiam orientalem* (Rome, 1947).
41. *Didachè* VIII, 4–10.

the prayers and rites, which we still find between the Lord's Prayer and communion and which are a certain obscuration of the whole, have been given an opportunity to be included in the Mass if Pope Gregory the Great had not moved the Lord's Prayer?

We think that it had been an expression of consistent liturgical view to place the fraction rite before the Lord's Prayer and omit the embolism, the private prayer of the priest, and the invitation formula. The rite of peace could then have its place at the beginning of the Liturgy of the Eucharist. This way we could experience the Lord's Prayer as an immediate preparation for communion and the essential link between the eucharistic prayer and communion would be better expressed.

The Rite of Peace

The renewed rite brings three elements together: the priest's prayer for peace with the Amen by the people, his greeting for peace facing the people who answer, and when appropriate, the gesture of peace given to one another. By bringing these elements together, this rite is more harmonious and clear compared with the rite in the Tridentine Missal. In the Missal of 1570 the prayer for peace came after the commingling (part of the host was dropped in the chalice during the embolism) and the *Agnus Dei* and was said in a low voice. The prayer for peace itself was said immediately after the embolism, during the commingling. With that, the exchange of peace took place but only among the clergy and only at a solemn Mass.

The rite of peace originally came after the Liturgy of the Word as a transition to the Liturgy of the Eucharist. Indeed, Justin Martyr mentions in his *Apologia* that a sign of peace was exchanged when the intercessions were ended and before the gifts for the Eucharist were brought in.[42] Tertullian calls the kiss of peace the seal of the prayer.[43] We find the same procedure in the *Traditio Apostolica* of Hippolytus: "And when he has been made bishop, all shall offer the kiss of peace, greeting him because he has been made worthy. Then the deacons will present the offering to him. . . ."[44] From the

42. Justinus, "Apologia I," 65, *PG* 6, k 427–428.
43. Tertullianus, "Liber de Oratione," c 8, *PL* 1, k 1176–1177.
44. Hippolytus, "*Traditio Apostolica*," 9. See also 18 and 21.

procession with the gifts that ensued after the kiss of peace, this rite was quickly understood as an application of the words from Matthew 5:23-24: "[G]o first and be reconciled with your brother, and then come and offer your gift."

While all Eastern and Western liturgies, including the Gallican, adopted the rite of peace at the beginning of the Liturgy of the Eucharist, a different development came about in the churches of North Africa and Italy. Over the course of the fourth century, the sign of peace became a rite of preparation for communion. Augustine was a witness to this in the church of North Africa when he wrote: "After the sanctification of the divine sacrifice has been effected, we say the Lord's Prayer, the prayer which you were taught and have recited. After that is said 'Peace be with you,' and the Christians kiss one another with a holy kiss. This is a sign of peace. Let what the lips express outwardly be also in the conscience, that is, as your lips draw near to your brother's, so let your heart not withdraw from his."[45]

For the Roman liturgy, this also seems to be normal in the beginning of the fifth century. A letter from Pope Innocent I in 416 to Bishop Decentius of Gubbio confirms this.[46] Here this kiss of peace, which was given when the *mysteria* were completed, still had the meaning of a consenting seal of the foregoing. It is only when Pope Gregory the Great let the Lord's Prayer follow immediately after the eucharist prayer and the kiss of peace after the embolism, that one could see in this kiss the ritual effect of the petition "forgive us our trespasses as we forgive those who trespass against us" in preparation for communion.

The bond with communion became so strong in the next period that one only wanted to give the kiss of peace to whoever would communicate.[47] Especially in the period when the frequency of communion began to fall sharply, one began to see the rite of peace as a substitute for communion. With the decline of regular communion, people who did not participate in receiving communion

---

45. Augustinus, "Sermo 227. Ad Infantes. De Sacramentis," *PL* 38, k 1101. English translation in Sheerin, *o.c.*, 98.

46. Innocentius I, "Epistula 25," I 4, *PL* 20, k 553.

47. In this sense, the rite of peace also occurred in the rite of communion for the sick in the Carolingian empire.

began to leave the church before Mass was ended. Caesarius of Arles (470–542) ordered all the faithful to remain in church at least "until the Lord's Prayer has been said and the people have received a blessing."[48] Gregory of Tours (538–594) explicitly speaks about the people "beginning to receive the most holy Body of the Redeemer after the dismissal."[49] We note here that the kiss of peace was a rite in which the entire community who remained participated. The kiss of peace was not passed from the celebrant to the faithful during this period, but everyone gave the kiss to whomever stood next to him or her.

Gradually a curious evolution occurred. According to the oldest manuscripts of the *Ordo Romanus I* the archdeacon still gave the kiss of peace to the first bishop, after which the others in order and also the people do the same (*deinde ceteri per ordinem et populus*). In the later manuscripts of this *Ordo*, this became: *at* the other in order and *at* the people (*deinde ceteris per ordinem et populis*). The sign of peace was thus transmitted hierarchically as a gift from the altar, with the faithful continuing to participate. When the liturgy evolved more and more into a clerical liturgy in which the faithful became silent and inactive spectators, however, the rite was limited to the clergy and then only in a solemn high Mass.

Within this development a prayer was made in which the priest addressed himself to Christ, who had promised peace to his church. The prayer originated in Germany at the beginning of the eleventh century. In this prayer, which is in the first person singular, the priest asks Christ not to pay attention to his sinful unworthiness, but to grant peace and unity because of the faith of his church.

Thus arose a rather complicated rite within the Roman liturgy. During the embolism, the priest took the paten, made a sign of the cross with the paten over himself, kissed it, and moved it under the host. Then he removed the pall from the chalice and broke the host in two while saying the words, "*Per eundem Dominum. . . .*" When he uttered the words "*Qui tecum vivit*" he broke a piece of

48. Caesarius of Arles, "Sermo 73," 2, *Corpus Christianorum Series Latina*, vol. 103 (Turnhout: Brepols, 1953) 307.

49. Gregorius Turronensis, *De virtutibus sancti Martini* II, 47, ed. Bruno Krusch, 626.

the left part of the host and held it in his hand during the *Per omnia saecula*. While saying the prayer of peace he made three crosses over the chalice with the piece of host. Then the rite of commingling followed whereby the priest dropped the particle of the host into the chalice and said the *Haec commixtio*. He prayed the *Agnus Dei* in silence and stroked his breast three times. After the prayer for peace, *Domine Jesu Christe*, said only in solemn Masses, he finally gave the kiss of peace. It was complicated, indeed!

The renewed rite of peace has become clearer, and the prayer is now said in the plural form. With the reforms of Vatican II, we might have returned to the older tradition, which the Eastern liturgy preserved, and placed the rite of peace at the beginning of the Liturgy of the Eucharist. Here, too, the medieval prayer for peace could disappear. If the Penitential Rite was also moved to the beginning of the Liturgy of the Eucharist, the rite of peace could become a meaningful event. In an admonition, we can point to the special aspect of the liturgical year or of the feast. In this way, we could avoid the danger of formalism that exists in stereotypically repeating the same formula.

Now that the church has opted for the preservation of the rite of peace in the same place as in the Missal of 1570, we might regret that the prayer for peace has been maintained. There does not seem to be any convincing argument that justifies the preservation of this prayer. First, the prayer dates only from the eleventh century, so the argument of loyalty to tradition is poor. Then, it is a prayer addressed to Christ, which is disturbing since all prayers in the Liturgy of the Eucharist address the Father. The prayer assumes that the *pax* comes from the altar along a hierarchical path to the faithful, while the rite of peace was both originally and within the renewal a mutual expression of love. One transformed an originally silent prayer of preparation of the priest into a presidential prayer. The singular "my sins" was changed into the plural "our sins," probably to promote the common character of the prayer. The original and meaningful opposition, "my sins . . . the faith of your Church" has been lost. Within the context in which the prayer arose, the priest could ask Christ not to look on his personal unworthiness, but to grant his peace to the church who believed in his promise. We are dealing here with a compromise solution: on the one hand, the preservation of the prayer was required, but on the other hand, the councilors tried to give it a new meaning.

It is positive, however, that the rite of peace is again a common and mutual ritual. It is no longer a privilege of the clergy in a solemn Mass, nor is it a gesture that follows a hierarchical path. On the contrary, the rite belongs to the faith community. The formula, "Let us offer each other a sign of peace" comes from the Ambrosian liturgy. According to the *Litterae circulares* of April 27, 1973, this is not an exclusive formula.[50] Thus, the priest can say another adapted admonition according to the character of the community.

The General Instruction does not prescribe a specific way to give the sign of peace, and the conferences of bishops have to establish this practice in accordance with the culture and customs of the peoples. The ICEL translation determines it as follows:

> According to what is decided by the Conference of Bishops, all express to one peace, communion, and charity. While the Sign of Peace is being given, it is permissible to say, The peace of the Lord be with you always, to which the reply is Amen. (GIRM 154)

Fraction Rite, Commingling and Agnus Dei

The Breaking of the Bread

The fraction rite is as old as the eucharistic celebration itself. At the Last Supper, in accordance with the Jewish meal rituals, Jesus took the bread into his hands while he said the thanksgiving, then broke the bread and gave it to his disciples to eat. Because of the words he uttered, this bread and the act of eating it acquired a very special meaning. This is what the four institution narratives report (Matt 26:26, Mark 14:22; Luke 22:19; 1 Cor 11:24). The two disciples going to Emmaus recognized Christ in his breaking of the bread (Luke 24:30-31). This breaking of the bread soon became the name to indicate the entire Eucharist.

Although it is not quite certain that the term "breaking of the bread" really refers to the eucharistic celebration, it is nevertheless remarkable that the first Christians in Jerusalem "devoted themselves . . . to the breaking of bread" (Acts 2:42). They were "breaking

---

50. "Eucharisticae participationem," *Notitiae* 9 (1973) 193–201, 199 n. 14.

bread in their homes" (Acts 2:46). When the church began to expand, it is mentioned: "On the first day of the week, when we gathered to break bread . . . " (Acts 20:7). We cannot misunderstand Paul's words: "The bread which we break, is it not a participation in the body of Christ?" (1 Cor 10:16). Christ himself is our slaughtered paschal lamb (1 Cor 5:7).

We find the expression *fractio panis* in the *Didache* from the end of the first century: "On the Lord's day come together, break bread and give thanks, having first confessed your transgressions, that your sacrifice may be pure" (14:1). Originally, the breaking of the bread was a practical necessity in view of distributing the eucharistic bread among the participants. Until the ninth century in the West, as still today in the East, they used leavened bread, which was broken for the communicating clergy and faithful. This fraction rite obviously took a long time when the congregation was large.

In the papal liturgy of the early Middle Ages, the pope goes to his *cathedra* after the kiss of peace, while the deacons carry the paten with two consecrated breads to him. In the meantime, the acolytes come to the altar with linen sacks in which the archdeacon puts the other consecrated loaves. The acolytes bring these to the concelebrating bishops and priests. On a sign from the pope all start the breaking of the bread. During this fraction, the *Agnus Dei* is sung, at least since Pope Sergius I (papacy 687–701) at the end of the seventh century.[51] In Gaul, the bread was shaped like a wreath so that by breaking off the pieces one received a round piece of bread, the primal shape of the later small hosts.

In the West from the ninth century on, when unleavened bread was used, and in the following centuries as the number of communicants declined sharply, only smaller pieces of bread were needed. The practical function of the breaking of the bread was thus lost. At that time, there was no distinction between the bread for the priest and the faithful. But in the thirteenth century the distinction between the great host for the celebrating priest and small hosts for the faithful arose. Something of the former fraction rite continued to exist, however, because initially the priest's host was broken into

51. M. Andrieu, *Les Ordines Romani II, o.c.,* 100–101.

three pieces: a piece for the commingling, a piece for the celebrant, and another piece broken in two for the deacon and the subdeacon or for the sick. This practice also disappeared as the priest began to consume two parts and used another part for the commingling. The breaking of bread lost its practical function as preparation for communion completely and was only seen in connection with the rite of commingling. In the following centuries, the whole of the rites between the Canon and communion developed into the opaque ritual of the Missal of 1570.

The fraction rite also has a symbolic meaning, which was pointed out from the beginning of the church. Paul wrote to the Christians of Corinth: "The bread that we break, is it not a participation in the body of Christ? Because the loaf of bread is one, we, though many, are one body, for we all partake of the one loaf" (1 Cor 10:16-17). In the *Didache*, we read: "As this broken bread was scattered over the mountains, and when brought together became one, so let your Church be brought together from the ends of the earth into your kingdom."[52]

In this and other explanations of breaking bread from the first centuries the symbolism of unity in multiplicity is always developed. The many fragments at the fraction rite remind us of the many grains that together form the one bread. When this one bread that has become the sacramental Body of Christ is again divided among the faithful, this expresses how all together they become the one ecclesial Body of Christ.

This rich symbolism would continue to be appealing as long as the breaking of the bread had a meaningful function in the eucharistic celebration. When the breaking had lost its purpose and was intended solely for the commingling, however, this gave rise to new symbolic explanations. So, for example, the three particles were associated with the fighting, suffering, and triumphant church. These and similar symbolic interpretations, however, distracted from the essential symbolism of the fraction rite.

Scientific liturgical studies in the twentieth century demonstrated the need for a reform of this rite. The suggestions formulated at

---

52. *Didachè* 9:4. Translation Jasper and Cuming, *o.c.*, 23.

the international liturgical congresses of the 1950s were seriously taken into account in forming the renewed liturgy. The 1970 Missal restored the fraction rite to its original place for the purpose of the communion. It recognizes not only the practical purpose but also refers to 1 Corinthians 10:17, noting the symbolism of the unity of the faithful with Christ through communion. It does not end with a statement of principle but provides guidelines for an effective rite:

> During the Agnus Dei (Lamb of God), the Deacons or some of the concelebrants may help the principal celebrant to break the hosts for Communion of both the concelebrants and the people. (GIRM 240)

More explicit is what is said about the bread that is needed for the eucharistic celebration:

> The bread for celebrating the Eucharist must be made only from wheat, must be recently made, and, according to the ancient tradition of the Latin Church, must be unleavened. (GIRM 320)

> By reason of the sign, it is required that the material for the Eucharistic Celebration truly have the appearance of food. Therefore, it is desirable that the Eucharistic Bread, even though unleavened and made in the traditional form, be fashioned in such a way that the Priest at Mass with the people is truly able to break it into parts and distribute these to at least some of the faithful. However, small hosts are not at all excluded when the large number of those receiving Holy Communion or other pastoral reasons call for them. Moreover, the gesture of the fraction or breaking of bread, which was quite simply the term by which the Eucharist was known in apostolic times, will bring out more clearly the force and importance of the sign of the unity of all in the one bread, and of the sign of charity by the fact that the one bread is distributed among the brothers and sisters. (GIRM 321)

The General Instruction clearly states that the hosts must have the appearance of real bread that can effectively be broken. We could interpret this as a rejection of the paper-thin white hosts and an approbation of the thicker brown communion wafers, which are more reminiscent of bread due to matter and color. In order to be more effective, however, the conferences of bishops should have been given the opportunity to allow the use of daily leavened bread in specific cases. Originally, indeed, the faithful brought ordinary bread from home. It was only in the ninth century that the church in the West began to suggest the use of unleavened bread, and this has been the general rule since the eleventh century. The motives that played a role in this and the later dispute with the East on this matter do not sufficiently justify the desire to stick so strongly to unleavened bread. How many of the faithful know the historical background of unleavened bread? Does the rich symbolism of the fraction rite not deserve the use of real, daily bread?

The General Instruction determines that the host must be manufactured in such a way that the priest can break it into parts and distribute these parts to at least some of the faithful. For ordinary parish practice, it seems most feasible for the priest to take a few larger wafers and break them over the paten during the fraction rite. The other smaller wafers are on this paten and the priest lays the broken larger wafers on them. In this way it becomes clearer that the eucharistic bread is broken and distributed among all. In any case, and here the General Instruction insists on it, the sense of breaking must be clear to the faithful. Unfortunately, we still see priests limiting the breaking to their own host if they have not already broken it during the consecration to show it to the faithful in a broad gesture. Do they not understand the meaning of the fraction rite?

Agnus Dei

Because of its place between the peace wish and the sign of peace, the *Agnus Dei* seemed to belong to the Rite of Peace in the former Missal, at least in the read Mass. The last petition of the *Agnus Dei* enhanced this impression. In the sung Mass, in which the choir sung the *Agnus Dei* while the priest, who had prayed it in silence, continued with the preparation for the communion, it seemed more like an accompanying song to communion. As such, the *Agnus Dei* had lost its original meaning in the former Missal.

The introduction of the *Agnus Dei* in the Roman liturgy is attributed to Pope Sergius I, who defined that it "should be sung by the clergy and the people during the breaking of the Lord's Body."[53]

---

53. L. Duchesne, *Le Liber pontificalis. Texte, introduction et commentaire* 1 (Paris, 1886) 376.

The *Agnus Dei* functioned as a *confractorium*, an accompanying song during the breaking of the bread, and was repeated as often as needed. Most likely there existed in that time varying songs as we still find them in the Ambrosian liturgy. In this assumption, Sergius I decided that the *Agnus Dei* would be sung instead of a varying *confractorium*. This pope, who was Syrian although born in Sicily, had taken this song from the Syrian liturgy.[54] The use of the word "lamb" denoting the eucharistic bread, the slaughtered Christ, already existed in the East, as is still the case in the Byzantine liturgy.

The *Agnus Dei* as a song accompanying the *fractio panis* originally belonged to the community. It could function as a hymn in which the faithful greeted and supplicated Christ as the slain Lamb of the new Passover. However, when the liturgies began to use more difficult melodies, the people were deprived of singing and the choir began to take over. From the eleventh century onward the celebrant prayed the *Agnus Dei* silently for himself, and it began to have an isolated existence. This was all the more the case because during this period the functional breaking of the bread was replaced by the use of small hosts, and the faithful received communion less and less. One saw the breaking of the bread only for the purpose of the commingling. Separated from its original function, the repetition of the *Agnus Dei* was reduced to the holy number three and ended up in the rite of peace. This led in the eleventh century to the transformation of the third petition into the *dona nobis pacem*.

Under the influence of the liturgical studies the *Agnus Dei* was restored as an accompanying chant during the breaking of the bread (GIRM 83). This restoration and the possibility to repeat it until the conclusion of this rite is an important element for active participation. Indeed, the first condition for the realization of active participation is the clarity of the rite.

Nevertheless, there are some reservations. Did it not make more sense, as in the oldest practice, to drop the appeal for peace and repeat only the appeal for mercy? As we have said, the appeal for peace originated only when the *Agnus Dei* became an element of the rite of peace. The retention of this appeal now means a doubling relative to the current rite of peace. But Pope Paul VI insisted on

---

54. Many Syrians fled in that time to the West because of the rise of Islam.

preserving *dona nobis pacem.* On January 1968 three forms of the so-called normative Mass were celebrated in the presence of the pope. At all three Masses the *Agnus Dei* ended with "have mercy on us." In his written remarks, the pope argued that the third acclamation of the Agnus Dei should not be changed.[55] Paul VI was extremely concerned about peace, as witnessed by his encyclical *Populorum Progressio*, his visit to the United Nations, and the establishment of an annual Day of Peace on January 1. In this sense, he wished to preserve the idea of peace, which had been associated with the *Agnus Dei* for many centuries. Yet it somewhat obscures the meaning of the *Agnus Dei* as *confractorium,* especially as it comes immediately after the rite of peace.

Because the *Agnus Dei* is an accompanying chant, it can only function when there is effectively a breaking of the bread and not in Masses in which only the priest's host is broken. To continue to use the *Agnus Dei* here makes the ritual less insightful and overloads the celebration. May we interpret the expression *de more* in article 83 of the General Instruction as saying that singing the *Agnus Dei* is not necessary when there is no real breaking of the bread? Would it have been a good idea to indicate the *Agnus Dei* not as exclusive *confractorium* but as one of the possible accompanying chants? In alternative hymns, we could develop the apostolic image of the one bread that is broken for all. Or, may we interpret the expression *de more* as, usually we sing *Agnus Dei* but other accompanying chants are not excluded?[56]

The Commingling

Although this rite occurs in one form or another in all ancient liturgies, it raises many questions for liturgical scholarship. The first time the rite seems to occur is in the Syrian liturgy, where Theodore

---

55. Annibale Bugnini, *The Reform of the Liturgy: 1948–1975* (Collegeville, MN: Liturgical Press, 1990) 365.

56. We find an opening in this direction in the *Directory for Masses with Children*: "To facilitate the children's participation in singing the Gloria, *Credo, Sanctus,* and *Agnus Dei,* it is permissible to use with the melodies appropriate vernacular texts, accepted by competent authority, even if these do not correspond exactly to the liturgical texts" (art. 31).

of Mopsuestia (350–428) mentions such a rite. He even describes two consecutive moments of commingling that have the same meaning for him:

> He [the bishop] traces the sign of the cross over the blood with the bread and over the bread with the blood. He brings them together as a sign that, though they are two distinct things, they are one in power and are the memorial of the passion and death that affected our Lord's body when he shed his blood on the cross for us all. . . . A human body is one with its blood, which is diffused throughout every part of it. That is why, wherever you make a cut, be it big or small, blood must flow from the place of the incision. This was true of our Lord's body before the passion . . . we set both bread and wine on the altar as a sign of what took place and as a reminder that the two are one in power, because both belong to the one who underwent the passion. . . . For this reason it is laid down that he [the bishop] should drop the life-giving bread piece by piece into the chalice. This action shows that the two elements are inseparable, that they are one in power and that they confer one and the same grace on the receiver.[57]

For Theodore of Mopsuestia the separate consecration of bread and wine represented the death of Christ as the separation of flesh and blood. The commingling or bringing together of both elements represented Christ's resurrection as his return to life. At the same time, he underscores that body and blood derive their power from the one Christ to whom they belong. Here Theodore gives a symbolic significance to a custom that probably goes back to the communion rite in household liturgies, where the first Christians took the sacred species home. Because leavened bread quickly becomes hard, before eating it they dipped it in wine or water to soften it. The manner in which communion is distributed in the Eastern liturgies—by immersing all of the consecrated bread into the chalice with the consecrated wine—probably goes back to this custom. The

---

57. Theodore of Mopsuestia, *Baptismal Homily V*, 15–17. Translation in: Edward Yarnold, *The Awe-Inspiring Rites of Initiation: Baptismal Homilies of the Fourth Century* (Slough: St. Paul Publications, 1972) 248–249.

faithful then received communion under both species, with the bread placed directly into their mouths by means of a spoon.

In the Western liturgy, the rite of commingling occurs in the papal Mass of the seventh and eighth centuries. Here we find two moments of commingling. The first happens just before the kiss of peace by the pope: while he makes three signs of the cross and pronounces the words of peace, he drops a portion of the consecrated bread into the chalice. This portion, called *sancta*, was kept from a previous eucharistic celebration and symbolized the continuity of the one sacrifice of Christ through successive celebrations. Originally, there was no such commingling in the papal Mass, but what did occur was that a part of the bread consecrated by the pope was taken to each of the seven titular churches of Rome, where the Eucharist was also celebrated. At the moment of the rite of peace, this particle, called *fermentum*, was mingled with the consecrated wine. This gesture expressed ecclesiastical unity, and it was precisely because of this symbolism that the commingling began to occur during the rite of peace. During the Middle Ages, however, the use of the *fermentum* disappeared, as did the *sancta*. At this place came another commingling that originally functioned elsewhere.

This other act of commingling occurred just before the pope received communion, whereby he dropped into the chalice a piece of the consecrated bread that he would consume. This commingling, probably inspired by the Syrian practice, symbolized the completeness of the Body and Blood of the glorified Christ. This second commingling eventually disappeared from this place in the Mass and came on the place of the first commingling. The expressiveness of the original commingling, however, weakened through the introduction of a probably different meaning.

The purpose of the rite became even more obscure in the Tridentine Missal with the use of the accompanying formula: "May this mingling and consecration of the Body and Blood of our Lord Jesus Christ be to us who receive it effectual unto eternal life. Amen." This formula, which originally did not mention the Body of Christ, came from another rite of commingling in connection with the wine. In the papal Mass, a portion of the consecrated wine was mingled with the unconsecrated wine that was waiting in chalices for the communion of the faithful. Due to the commingling of the consecrated and the unconsecrated wine, the latter was also considered to be consecrated: *consecratio per contactum*. This rite of commingling disappeared when the faithful no longer received communion from the chalice, but the accompanying formula remained and caused confusion by the use of the word *consecratio*.

We may regret that the new Order of Mass has retained the commingling. It remains completely incomprehensible to most, as the laypeople who were present in the experimental celebration of the normative Mass in January 1968 said.[58] The positive view is that this rite, together with the fraction rite, has been removed from the rite of peace and placed immediately before communion. As a result, each statement lapses as if this rite symbolized the continuity of the eucharistic celebration or its unity. By putting the rite of commingling back before communion, understanding this rite by using the symbolism of the completeness of the risen Lord becomes possible again.

Yet do we need a rite to express this fact? The only reason to maintain commingling may be an ecumenical consideration since it is highly appreciated in the Eastern liturgies. This argument played an important role in the deliberations of *coetus* 10. Dom Bernard Botte thought the most acceptable allegorical explanation is to see in it a sign of the paschal mystery: the separate state of both species symbolizes Christ's suffering, while the commingling expresses his resurrection.[59] This explanation is what the General Instruction seems to accept when it says that the aim of the commingling is "to signify the unity of the Body and Blood of the Lord in the work of salvation, namely, of the Body of Jesus Christ, living and glorious" (GIRM 83).

More than arguing against the retention of the commingling rite, we can raise objections against the retention of the accompanying formula. This formula is irrelevant because it originated in a completely different context. The formula has been adapted by omitting the Amen and especially the words *et consecratio* so that any suggestion of a *consecratio per contactum* is avoided.

---

58. "The rite of the commingling was not understood; it could even suggest the erroneous idea of consecration by contact." Bugnini, *o.c.*, 368.

59. A.M. Franquesa, "Hoe is de nieuwe *Ordo Missae* tot stand gekomen?," *Tijdschrift voor Liturgie* 55 (1968) 5–24, 22.

Our conclusion about the fraction rite, *Agnus Dei,* and commingling can therefore be brief. The restoration of the fraction rite as immediate preparation for communion, as well as the revaluation of the *Agnus Dei* as an accompanying song during the fraction rite, to be sung by the congregation, are both positive elements of the renewed liturgy. What may not be as positive is keeping the commingling rite, especially with the accompanying formula. Further, it is desirable that, in addition to the *Agnus Dei,* other accompanying hymns that express unity through receiving communion would be admitted to the liturgy. At the same time, there should be the freedom to omit this song if there is no effective gesture of breaking bread.

Communion

The Personal Preparation of the Priest

The General Instruction says that the priest prepares himself for communion in silent prayer, while the faithful can do the same. The Order of Mass provides two prayers from which the priest must choose. These prayers have been taken from the former Missal, where both were prayed.[60] Furthermore, the closing formula of both prayers, "who with the same God the Father, in the unity of the Holy Spirit, lives and reigns God, for ever and ever. Amen" is now dropped. In the second prayer the phrase "Which I, unworthy, presume to receive" is omitted. On the other hand, the drinking of the Blood is added to the eating of the Body (*perceptio Corporis et Sanguinis*).

The first prayer stems from the Carolingian era and was first found in the Sacramentary of Amiens (ninth century). The second prayer was in the Sacramentary of Fulda (tenth century). Other preparatory prayers also originated in this time. Even though Bernold of Constance around 1090 seemed to oppose the expansion of these prayers, which were not official but stemmed from pious tradition, an expansion did occur.

We can situate the insertion of these prayers into the liturgy within the flourishing period of the apologies, confessions of the guilt and

---

60. In fact, they were the second and third of the priest's preparatory prayers. The first was that what today introduces the rite of peace ("Lord Jesus Christ, you said. . .").

unworthiness of the celebrant. It was also the period when communion by the faithful went back to the absolute minimum, and communion during the eucharistic celebration became a matter for the celebrant alone. The priest then prepared himself with these private prayers. The prayers promoted the separation between the celebrant and faithful. Based on the history of these prayers, we may regret that the new Missal has kept them. Moreover, these prayers are addressed to Christ and not to the Father. In this sense, they disturb the usual prayer orientation of the Eucharist.

In the renewal of the rite of communion, the councilors undoubtedly wanted to start from the communal character of this rite, that is, to gather the faith community as one family around the eucharistic table. Based on that principle, why were these private prayers retained? The only explanation is that perhaps this was a compromise with those who wished to change as little as possible. As such, these prayers did not completely disappear, rather, a choice was given to pray one of the prayers.

In order to ensure a communal aspect, the councilors added that the faithful also had to prepare themselves in silence for communion. This preparatory prayer of the faithful, however, is not an innovation. In the early Middle Ages we find collections of preparatory prayers for the faithful. From private devotional practice these prayers ended up in the Mass texts, where in the period of the decline in communion of the faithful they became private prayers for the celebrant.

For the few times that the faithful received communion, a separate cycle of preparatory prayers arose at the end of the Middle Ages. These were taken from the rite for the communion of the sick. Here especially the *Confiteor* earned great significance as a preparatory prayer for the faithful. This rite was not in the Missal but in the *Rituale Romanum.*

In the years before Vatican II, this practice started to seem illogical, especially when the faithful began to receive communion immediately after the priest. The *Codex Rubricarum* of 1960 abolished the *Confiteor* before the communion of the faithful.[61] This abolition and the integration of communion raises the question of whether

---

61. "Codex Rubricarum, " *AAS* 52 (1960) 597–685, 680.

the same motive should apply to the private prayers of the priest. Are these private prayers, said just before the culmination of the unitary experience of communion, not one of those repetitions that should be avoided? Immediately after the private prayers of the priest, the faithful and the priest together make an act of humility by praying, "Lord, I am not worthy . . ." Isn't this prayer sufficient and more appropriate to communion?

The Invitation to Receive Communion and the Act of Humility

> Then the Priest shows the faithful the Eucharistic Bread, holding it over the paten or over the chalice, and invites them to the banquet of Christ; and along with the faithful, he then makes an act of humility, using the prescribed words from the Gospels. (GIRM 84)

The invitation consists of two biblical quotations. The first is the cry of John the Baptist pointing his followers to Jesus as the Lamb of God (John 1:29). This text was used in the ritual for communion since the sixteenth century and relates in substance to the *Agnus Dei*. In a certain sense it is a warning not to receive communion lightly. We can compare this expression with the Byzantine formula *ta hagia tois hagiois* (holy things to the holy), which we find also in the old Gallican liturgy (*sancta sanctis*).

In *coetus* 10 it was suggested that the formula *sancta sanctis* be used, which is much older than *Ecce Agnus Dei* and could be interpreted as an ecumenical element. The majority thought that the formula *Ecce Agnus Dei* did not need to be changed, however, especially since it was combined with the eschatological *Beati qui ad cenam Agni Dei vocati sunt*, "Blessed are those called to the supper of the Lamb." Where the expression *ta hagia tois hagiois* simultaneously contained an invitation and a warning, *ecce Agnus Dei* could function as a warning, but not as much as an invitation.

The addition of *Beati qui ad cenam Agni Dei vocati sunt* makes it an explicit invitation. This sentence is new in the eucharistic liturgy. It is taken from Revelation 19:9 and immediately puts communion in an eschatological perspective. We celebrate the Eucharist as a pledge of the final bridal meal with the Lamb. This is, indeed, somewhat difficult to understand and presupposes a more biblically educated congregation. That may be why some translations, including the one from ICEL, first translated this as, "Happy are those who are called to his supper." Taking into account the mandate of the Roman document *Liturgiam authenticam*, we now have a more literal translation. This makes the connection to Scripture clearer. It also makes clearer the necessity of opportunities for the biblical and liturgical education of our faithful.

After the invitation, the faithful and the priest pray as one community: "Lord, I am not worthy that you should enter under my roof, but only say the word and my soul shall be healed." This is an adaptation based on the words of the centurion in Matthew 8:8 and Luke 7:6-7, and is a formula that was used as preparatory prayer for communion since the tenth century. Although originally it was said only once, over time people began to say it three times while gently striking the chest. The renewed liturgy prescribes saying it only once. This not only avoids routine and the danger of rattling off the text but also stresses the meaning of this prayer. Indeed, it is not an acclamation or an invocation that benefits from repetition, but a humble acknowledgment of our unworthiness to sit at the celestial supper. This formula retains the essence of the previous ICEL text, "Lord, I am not worthy to receive you, but only say the word and I shall be healed," but the literal translation used today helps us have the same attitude as the centurion as we prepare to receive Christ into our very selves.

With regard to active participation, the renewal of this rite is most welcome.

Communion of the Celebrant

It is remarkable that the General Instruction in article 85 points to the importance that the faithful, just like the priest, "receive the Lord's Body from hosts consecrated at the same Mass and that, in the cases where this is foreseen, they partake of the chalice . . . "

From the principle that the celebrant acts *in persona Christi* it is self-evident that he is the first and, in a small community, the only one who distributes communion. In a certain sense, this symbolizes that Christ himself gives the people of God, whom he called together, his Body and Blood to eat and drink. This is an important factor that benefits the clarity of the eucharistic celebration and thereby promotes active participation. In any case, this is a major improvement over previous practice, in which the celebrant received communion during "his" Mass, while the faithful who wanted to receive could go to another priest who gave them hosts from the tabernacle.

It is also significant that the celebrant is the first to receive. This expresses that, as their presider, he also represents the gathered faith community. In Masses without the faithful, the celebrant communicates not only in his own name, but as the representative of the people of God. Receiving communion is an act of engagement. In faith and gratitude we acknowledge and receive the Lord in his total self-giving for our salvation, and enter into his paschal mystery. We are transformed into the living Body of Christ on earth, the church. As church, we grow in fraternal love and commitment to the world according to the desire of God, who by our actions is fully glorified. Whoever takes bread and wine as presider and interprets them in the eucharistic prayer as the Body and Blood of Christ, must also be the first to express his willingness to enter into Christ's paschal mystery. There he can be guided by the unifying Spirit to rewrite Christ's gospel for all men and women. When the presider is the first to receive Communion, it does not mean that we want to give him a place of honor here.[62]

We may question why the two prayers the priest says while consuming the two species have been retained, although shortened to their essential form. The Amen has been omitted from both prayers; the *animam meam* has been changed to "me" and the *Domini nostri Iesu Christi* has been simplified to *Christi*. These prayers were originally formulas that accompanied the dispensing of communion to the faithful. Originally, it was one formula for communion under both forms. From the eleventh century on it was split into two, one for each of the forms. Where one would expect the communicant to answer "Amen," the priest also said this, because in this period communion was received on the tongue. Where initially the priest communicated without the accompanying formula, the tendency

---

62. It is important to underscore this because modern sensibilities might suggest that it is better that the priest, as the person in office, should first serve the people. It is also important to safeguard the symbolic significance against the practical consideration that when the priest should first serve the people he could consume the remaining hosts and the residue of the chalice without communicating twice.

arose to say these prayers at his communion. When the communion of the faithful disappeared more and more, the two prayers, one for each form, became private prayers and ended up in the Pius V Missal.

For the communion of the faithful the new Missal has opted for a very old and meaningful formula, "The Body (Blood) of Christ," to which the faithful answer, "Amen." It is a pity that this formula is not also used for the communion of the priest, of course without the Amen, because a different formula for priest and faithful maintains the distinction between the two. In terms of content, the old formula is much richer in its brevity. Where the formula for the communion of the priest is an optative formula for the fruits of communion— "May the Body (Blood) of Christ keep me safe for eternal life"—the formula used by the people is an effective creed of the faithful who want to receive the consecrated gifts as Body and Blood of Christ.

Communion of the Faithful

Communion from Hosts Consecrated at the Same Mass. In article 85, the General Instruction clearly determines:

> It is most desirable that the faithful, just as the Priest himself is bound to do, receive the Lord's Body from hosts consecrated at the same Mass and that, in the cases when this is foreseen, they partake of the chalice (cf. no. 283), so that even by means of the signs Communion will stand out more clearly as a participation in the sacrifice actually being celebrated.

In ancient times, when the faithful themselves brought the gifts from home for the celebration of the Eucharist, it was evident that they also received these as consecrated gifts. A part of the consecrated bread was kept for the sick, a custom from which the reserved sacrament came into being.

When the frequency of sacramental communion declined in the late Middle Ages and was preserved almost only for the priest, the faithful opted for what one began to call "spiritual communion." The decline of sacramental communion cannot be explained solely by indolence or indifference, since in monastic communities too receiving communion was restricted to at most a few times a year. During the struggle against Arianism, the church emphasized Christ's divinity in perhaps too one-sided a manner. This gave rise to a diffident attitude towards communion.

Changes in the practice of penance as well as the obligation of prior confession and the requirement that married couples abstain from sexual intercourse before receiving communion also reduced the frequency of communion. People at liturgy made a grateful reflection on Christ's redemptive suffering and his offering on the cross as perpetuated in every Mass. Then they united with Christ at the communion of the priest through the acts of faith, hope, and love. Moreover, some theologians argued that the priest communicated on behalf of the entire congregation, and that the faithful, therefore, were excused from receiving the sacrament, provided that the faithful united spiritually with the eucharistic event. The eucharistic movement that started at the end of the twelfth century especially promoted this spiritual communion in the adoration of the Blessed Sacrament.

Currents that favored more frequent sacramental communion arose against this practice. During the Reformation, an extreme reaction claimed that Masses in which only the priest communicates sacramentally were illegitimate. The Council of Trent (1545–1563) condemned this extreme position, but also encouraged the faithful to not only communicate spiritually but also sacramentally in order to participate fully in the eucharistic celebration.[63] After the Council, however, little account was actually taken of this incentive. Even more, priests who were concerned about promoting the sacramental communion of the faithful and gave them hosts that were consecrated in the Mass at which they were present, were considered suspect.

Pope Benedict XIV (papacy 1740–1758), in his encyclical *Certiores effecti* of 1742,[64] recommended that the faithful communicate not only spiritually but also sacramentally at the liturgical moment of communion, with hosts consecrated in the same Mass at which they participated. Attendees at the Synod of Pistoia (1786)[65] also

---

63. Conc. Trid. Sessio XXII caput VIII. www.thecounciloftrent.com/ch22.htm.

64. *Certiores effecti* in *Sanctissimi Domini Nostri Benedicti Papae XIV Bullarium*, 13 parts (Mechelen: 1826–1827), part I, 439–442.

65. C.A. Bolton, *Church Reform in 18th Century Italy: The Synod of Pistoia 1786* (The Hague: 1969).

endeavored for the active participation of the faithful in sacramental communion.[66] And the so-called Neo-Gallican liturgies (1667–1875) opted for the restoration of the communion of the faithful as part of the eucharistic celebration.[67]

Despite these movements to re-engage the faithful in receiving communion, the practice remained what it had been for several centuries. Only in the twentieth century, the liturgical movement, according to the desire of Pope Pius X (papacy 1903–1914) for active participation in the liturgy and his call for frequent communion, began to endeavor for the communion of the faithful. This would occur immediately after the celebrant's communion and with hosts consecrated in the Mass at which the faithful participated as actively as possible. The liturgical movement received a clear confirmation of its efforts in the encyclical *Mediator Dei et Hominum* (1947) of Pope Pius XII (1939–1958). In it the pope refers to the encyclical of Benedict XIV and in turn recommends the practice of having the faithful communicate at the proper liturgical moment, with hosts consecrated in the same Mass. At the same time, Pius XII noted they "really and truly take part in the sacrifice, should they receive a host which has been duly consecrated at a previous Mass."[68] The Constitution on the Sacred Liturgy of Vatican II, in article 55, strongly recommended that the faithful "receive the Lord's Body from the same sacrifice . . . " The instruction *Eucharisticum mysterium* of 1967 stated the same.[69] Ultimately, the General Instruction also emphasized the desirability of this practice.

In the renewed liturgy, the communion of the faithful takes place at the appropriate moment. The General Instruction assumes that the normal practice is that the priest consecrate at least a sufficient number of hosts during the Mass itself and give these to the faithful.

---

66. Cf. article 45 of the 57 that are discussed at this Synod. Scipio dei Ricci, bishop of Pistoia, promoted the publication of books dealing with the liturgical education of the faithful. About sacramental communion by the faithful see G. Nannaroni, *Del pubblico divin diritto alla communione eucaristica nel sacrifizio della messa* (Lugano: 1774).

67. Jozef Lamberts, "Een interessante bladzijde uit de liturgiegeschiedenis: de neo-gallicaanse liturgieën," *Tijdschrift voor Liturgie* 79 (1995) 197–209.

68. "Mediator Dei et hominum," *AAS* 39 (1947) 521–595, 564, n. 118.

69. "Eucharisticum mysterium," *AAS* 59 (1967) 539–573, n. 31.

In its description of what is to be prepared on the credence table, the General Instruction mentions the bread for the communion of the priest who presides, the ministers, and the people, unless this is presented by the faithful in procession at the offertory (GIRM 118). Practically, this means that it is against the liturgical sense when the priest leaves the altar after he receives communion to get a ciborium from the tabernacle with formerly consecrated hosts. The reservation of the Blessed Sacrament is meant for the communion of the sick and other pious purposes as blessing and eucharistic adoration. It should only be used at Mass if there is an insufficient estimate of the number of communicants. When the celebrant perceives that more faithful are present than expected, the fraction rite can offer a solution with the priest breaking the great hosts and some smaller hosts into small pieces.

Despite the teaching of Trent—that communion with formerly consecrated hosts gives full participation in the sacrifice and remains valid—the clarity of the rite and the fullness of the sign demand the faithful to communicate as much as possible with hosts that are consecrated in the celebration at which they participate. Wanting to promote the active participation of the faithful but deny them such communion is almost a contradiction in terms. The excuse that practical difficulties would prevent this only proves that one has insufficiently understood the liturgical and theological meaning of communion.

Communion under Both Kinds. Under the title "Some General Norms for all Forms of Mass," the General Instruction declares:

> Holy Communion has a fuller form as a sign when it takes place under both kinds. For in this form the sign of the Eucharistic banquet is more clearly evident and clearer expression is given to the divine will by which the new and eternal Covenant is ratified in the Blood of the Lord, as also the connection between the Eucharistic banquet and the eschatological banquet in the Kingdom of the Father. (GIRM 281)

In article 55 the Constitution on the Sacred Liturgy had suggested at first that communion under both kinds be reserved only for special occasions. We must place this against the historical background at the time of the Council of Trent. Since the twelfth century, the faithful's participation in communion with the chalice declined in the Latin church. This was supported by dogmatic considerations that, *per concomitantiam*, the entire Christ is present under each of the two kinds.[70] However, in the fifteenth century the followers of John Huss (1369–1415) made the lay chalice a confessional symbol based on John 6:53 ("Amen, amen, I say to you, unless you eat the flesh of the Son of Man and drink his blood, you do not have life within you.").

After initial resistance at the Council of Constance (1414–1418) and many subsequent complications, Pope Eugene IV (papacy 1431–1447) allowed the lay chalice to be given in Bohemia in 1433. In 1462 Pope Pius II (papacy 1458–1464), however, withdrew this permission. Many returned to the practice of communion under one kind, but others continued to endeavor for the lay chalice. In the sixteenth century, the Lutheran reform movement saw communion under one kind, as was the practice of Catholics then, as unfaithfulness to the Lord's command. German Catholics believed that allowing or not allowing the lay chalice was only a disciplinary measure and not a dogmatic standpoint. That is why they asked that the lay chalice be allowed in their regions in order to deprive the reformers of an important dogmatic argument.

The issue of the lay chalice was dealt with in the twenty-first session (July 1562) of the Council of Trent, which took a radical stand against the dogmatic assertions of the reformers. The dogmatic position of the Council of Trent consists of four points: (1) laypeople and clerics, when not sacrificing, are not bound, of divine right, to communion under both species; (2) communion under both species is not necessary for salvation; (3) the church has the power to make changes in the dispensation of the sacraments, their substance being untouched; and (4) Christ whole and entire and a true sacrament is received under either species alone. Once this dogmatic statement was made, whether or not to allow the lay chalice remained a purely disciplinary measure.

---

70. This was already pointed out by Anselm of Laon (1117) and William of Champeaux (1121).

The Council fathers in Trent, however, did not come to a decision about allowing the lay chalice for the German Catholics. Eventually they decided to leave the decision to the pope, and in 1564, Pope Pius IV (papacy 1559–1565) granted the archbishops of Cologne, Trier, Mainz, Salzburg, and Graz permission to introduce communion under both species. In the meantime, the long period of hesitation before a decision was made had caused the issue of the lay chalice to become a confessional sign of distinction for the Reformation. The Catholics in Germany themselves interpreted it in this way and resisted it, and in 1571, Pope Pius V (1566–1572) withdrew permission for receiving from the chalice.

In our time, the ideological and dogmatic background present in the time of Trent, which would prevent the introduction of the lay chalice, has disappeared. When liturgists in the years prior to Vatican II endeavored for the restoration of communion under both species, this was not motivated by the conviction that such communion is necessary but that, in this way, the fullness of the sign could be expressed. They did not want to urge communion under both species for every eucharistic celebration but wanted the church to say clearly that it is not a matter of principle to refuse communion under both species. They hoped that for well-defined cases the church would make it possible for the faithful to remember the experience of the Last Supper in full.

In article 55, the Constitution on the Sacred Liturgy mentioned a few cases for the admission of the lay chalice. The decree of March 7, 1965 increased the number of cases, but for the ordinary faithful it was actually limited to a wedding Mass or jubilee.[71] An extension was given again by the instruction *Eucharisticum Mysterium* of 1967, *Sacramentali Communione* of June 29, 1970,[72] and the General Instruction of the Roman Missal of 1975 (second edition).[73]

Article 283 of the General Instruction of the Roman Missal of 2002 (third edition) stipulates:

71. "Decretum generale 'Ritus concelebrationis et communionis sub utraque species' promulgantur," *AAS* 57 (1965) 410–412.

72. "Instructio de Cultu Mysterii Eucharistici," *AAS* 59 (1967) 539–573. "Sacramentali Communione," *AAS* 62 (1970) 664–667.

73. Art. 242.

The Diocesan Bishop may establish norms for Communion under both kinds for his own diocese, which are also to be observed in churches of religious and at celebrations with small groups. The Diocesan Bishop is also given the faculty to permit Communion under both kinds whenever it may seem appropriate to the Priest to whom a community has been entrusted as its own shepherd, provided that the faithful have been well instructed and that there is no danger of profanation of the Sacrament or of the rite's becoming difficult because of the large number of participants or for some other cause.

Regarding the way of distributing the Communion under both kinds to the faithful and the extension of the permission, the Conferences of Bishops may promulgate norms after approval of the decisions by the Apostolic See.

In 1984 the Apostolic See approved the 1978 resolution of the USCCB permitting the reception of communion under both kinds. With that, the ICEL translation changed the last paragraph of article 283 to read:

> In all that pertains to Communion under both kinds, the Norms for the Distribution and Reception of Holy Communion under Both Kinds in the Dioceses of the United States of America are to be followed (particularly nos. 27–54).[74]

This marks the accomplishment of an important goal of the liturgical movement, that is, the almost total restoration of communion under both kinds. The introduction of communion under both kinds presupposes the preparation of the faithful by an appropriate catechesis. Already the instruction *Sacramentali Communione* of June 29, 1970 underscored the necessity of catechesis explaining the significance of this rite.[75] It would be a pity if the faithful experienced communion under both kinds as a mere novelty. We must clearly point out that the lay chalice is not at all the satisfaction of an urge for novelty, but the reintroduction of an original practice. On the one hand, we must state that participation in the eucharistic meal is always a genuine

---

74. See *This Holy and Living Sacrifice: Directory for the Celebration and Reception of Communion under Both Kinds*, Part III.

75. "Sacramentali Communione," *AAS* 62 (1970) 664–667, 665.

communion with the Lord, regardless of whether this happens under one or both forms. On the other hand, we must clearly point out that communion under both kinds is a more complete sign, has a greater power of expression, and corresponds to the basic form of the Eucharist. In line with the elements of article 281, the priest may recall that the cup refers to the new and eternal covenant that is ratified in the Blood of the Lord. He can also show that drinking from the cup expresses the fundamental willingness of a Christian to unite with Christ, who has indeed drunk the bitter cup (Mark 10:38; Mark 14:36) by being ready to sacrifice his life for the redemption of all. In this way we can experience communion as the summit of active participation.

The Formula for Distributing Communion. About the reception of communion, the Order of Mass says:

> After this he [the priest] takes the paten or other vessel and goes to the communicants. The priest or other minister distributing the eucharistic bread takes a host for each communicant, raises it a little, and shows it, saying: *The body of Christ.* The communicant answers: *Amen* and receives communion. If any are receiving in both kinds, the rite described elsewhere is followed. When he presents the chalice, the minister says: *The blood of Christ.* The communicant answers: *Amen* and drinks it.

This short, ancient dialogue, which we find especially discussed in the works of Augustine, is an important element of active participation. What the minister shows to the faithful is the sacramental sign of Christ's presence offered to the communicant. The formula indicates in one breath both his eucharistic and his ecclesial presence. When the faithful then answer "Amen," this is a true confession of faith in and entrance to the presence of the Lord both in this sacrament and in his church. Ambrose of Milan explains the formula:

> When you approach, the priest says to you "The body of Christ" and you answer "Amen," that is, "True." What the tongue confesses let the heart hold fast.[76]

---

76. Ambrose, "De sacramentis, Liber IV c. 5,25," *PL* 16, k. 445. Sheerin, *o.c.*, 80. See also Cyrillus Hier., "Catecheses Mystagogicae Quinque IV 3," *PG* 33, k. 1099, *o.c.* 65.

This "Amen" not only expresses the communicant's faith in the eucharistic presence of the Lord, but also his or her willingness to build up the Body of Christ that is the church by participating in the eucharistic Body of Christ. By communicating in Christ, the head of the church as body, we also communicate with each other as members of this body. We are committed to working with and like Christ in mutual love, and quest for unity in order to realize his body, the church. Augustine testified:

> If, then, you wish to understand the body of Christ, listen to the Apostle as he says to the faithful "You are the body of Christ, and His members." If, therefore, you are the body of Christ and His members, your mystery has been placed on the Lord's Table, you receive your mystery. You reply "Amen" to that which you are, and by replying you consent. For you hear "The Body of Christ" and you reply "Amen." Be a member of the body of Christ so that your "Amen" may be true.[77]

Because this brief dialogue at communion as a personal profession of faith and as the expression of our readiness for Christian engagement is a unique moment of active participation, the minister should take the time to show the host to each communicant and say clearly "The Body of Christ," and give him or her the opportunity to answer "Amen." The faithful are no longer passive people who allow the priest to wish them a fruitful communion. They are active people who confess their faith and express their commitment to the eucharistic Christ. This moment is also an excellent starting point for eucharistic and ecclesial catechesis. Unfortunately, too often this opportunity for an interpretative and motivating catechesis remains unused in parochial practice.

The Act of Communion. The USCCB defined what is said in the official Latin text of the General Instruction as such:

> The norm established for the Dioceses of the United States of America is that Holy Communion be received standing, unless an individual member of the faithful wishes to receive Communion while kneeling. (Congregation for Divine Worship and the Discipline of the Sacraments, Instruction, *Redemptionis Sacramentum*, March 25, 2004, no. 91)

---

77. Augustinus, "Sermo 272," *PL* 38, k.1247. Sheerin, *o.c.*, 95.

When receiving Holy Communion, the communicant bows his or her head before the Sacrament as a gesture of reverence and receives the Body of the Lord from the minister. The consecrated host may be received either on the tongue or in the hand, at the discretion of each communicant. When Holy Communion is received under both kinds, the sign of reverence is also made before receiving the Precious Blood. (GIRM 160)

The General Instruction continues as follows:

If Communion is given only under the species of bread, the Priest raises the host slightly and shows it to each, saying The Body of Christ. The communicant replies, Amen, and receives the Sacrament either on the tongue or, where this is allowed, in the hand, the choice lying with the communicant. As soon as the communicant receives the host, he or she consumes the whole of it.

If, however, Communion is given under both kinds, the rite prescribed in nos. 284–287 is followed. (GIRM 161)

After an inquiry with the world episcopate about the desirability of communion in the hand had shown that opinions were divided, the instruction *Memoriale Domini* of May 29, 1969 provided that the conferences of bishops could submit an application to introduce communion in the hand in addition to communion on the tongue.[78]

Communion in the hand is not an innovation but a very old way of accepting the eucharistic bread. It is certain that Christ took the bread, broke it, and distributed it, placing it in the hands of his disciples at the Last Supper. If it were different, this would have mentioned by the evangelists. Cyril of Jerusalem (313–386) gives us an explicit description of communion in the hand and how we should experience it:

Coming up to receive, then, do not extend your hands with palm upward and your fingers spread, but making your left hand a throne for the right, for it is about to receive a king, and cupping your palm, receive the Body of Christ, and answer "Amen." Carefully hallow

---

78. "Memoriale Domini. Instructio de modo sanctum communionem ministrandi," *Notitiae* 5 (1969) 347–351.

your eyes through contact with the sacred body; then take it into your mouth, taking care to lose no part of it. If you were to lose part of it, it would be like losing one of your own members. Tell me, if someone gave you some flakes of gold, would you not take the greatest care to hold it fast, so as not to lose any of it and endure its loss? How much more carefully, then, will you guard against losing so much as a crumb of that which is more precious than gold or precious stones? Then after receiving the body of Christ, approach his blood. . . . "[79]

After the consecrated bread was laid in the right hand, people communicated by bending over and eating the particle with their mouth. From the ninth century onwards, people began to receive communion on the tongue, after this had been customary for some time in the rite for communion of the sick. The Synod of Rouen (878) determined clearly: "The Eucharist is not to be placed in the hands of any layman or laywoman but only in their mouths."[80] A reason for this change could have been the prevention of abuses, as some people did not eat the host but took it with them for superstitious practices. It was also the time when unleavened bread was introduced. Out of fear, then, that tiny crumbs could fall and be deconsecrated it seemed better to place the host directly on the tongue.

From the second millennium on, as we have noted before, not only did communion by the faithful decrease, but the entire liturgy became more and more a clerical affair. The priest was seen more and more as the one who was ordained to perform the liturgical rites. With regard to communion this was reflected in the belief that only his anointed hands were allowed to touch the hosts. This was probably influenced by a desire to assure due reverence for the sacred Body of Christ.

This practice led also to the custom of the faithful kneeling to receive communion. In the first centuries Christians received communion while standing. This was the normal posture for prayer in the East and it obtained a specific meaning for Christians in the

79. Cyrillus Hier., "Catecheses Mystagogicae Quinque, V 21," PG 33, k. 1124–1126.

80. J.D. Mansi, *Sacrorum Conciliorum nove et amplissima collectio*, pars. X (Florence: 1759) 1199.

West: through our baptism we participate in the risen Lord through communion. This posture of standing remained normative during the early Middle Ages. But when the practice of communion on the tongue became the norm, kneeling made it easier for the priest to put the host in people's mouths. At the same time, kneeling was then seen as an expression of reverence. This fit well in a period when the presence of the Lord under the species of bread and wine was almost regarded as an end in itself.

Quite soon, a linen cloth was held in front of the kneeling faithful to catch any crumbs or falling hosts. From the thirteenth century on, communion rails began to appear with increasing frequency. This arose from the Fourth Lateran Council (1215), which wanted the Blessed Sacrament to be kept from any abuse or irreverent approach. Churches then began to screen off the area of the church used by the lay congregation (the nave) from the chancel, which was used by the clergy. This led to the building of enormous rood screens with images of the crucifixion. When the Counter-Reformation wanted the congregation to have a better view of what the priest was doing at the altar, these screens were largely taken down and the low communion rail generally became the only barrier between the priest and the congregation. Communicants received the host on their tongue while kneeling at the communion rail, with both hands lifted up underneath a long white cloth attached at the communion rail or while passing a communion-plate from one communicant to the other.[81]

The liturgical renewal restored both communion in the hand and receiving while standing. Communion on the tongue and kneeling remain possible for people who prefer this. In 1969, in every respect, this was the correct pastoral decision. One could not simply abolish a practice linked with such special meaning for the faithful.[82] It was

---

81. GIRM article 118 seems still to suggest the use of a communion-plate when it mentions, under the items that should be prepared on the credence table, "the Communion-plate for the Communion of the faithful." According to article 287 this is to be used for communion by intinction.

82. The idea that only the priest may touch the host with his hands because his hands are anointed seemed to be very deeply rooted in many people. From their upbringing, many felt that accepting the host in the hand was less respectful than receiving it on the tongue. How many people were told as kids at their First Communion that they could not even touch the host with their teeth? How strong was the belief that kneeling is more respectful than standing?

necessary to provide the faithful with proper catechesis on the reasons for this "new" norm. Today, fifty years later, most of the faithful only know communion as received in the hand while standing.

We might ask whether the liturgical renewal has not brought a certain nonchalance for some people in receiving communion. We must point out that the "Amen" of the faithful who receive can nevertheless be a clear form of respect and appreciation. Standing is essentially the accepted attitude of respect by the faithful, who also stand during the gospel, the Creed and the eucharistic prayer (in some cases). The personal acceptance of the Body of Christ in the hand is also essentially a much more active form of reverence and recognition than the passive reception on the tongue. Liturgical catechesis must continue to underscore this, while in our liturgical practice we must ensure that communion is received in dignity and does not become a casual gesture.

In the first years of liturgical renewal, here and there a habit arose to pass the communion bowl with hosts from one to another. In a letter of June 6, 1969, the Congregation for Divine Worship provided for this possibility.[83] This was not confirmed anywhere else, however, and the practice was expressly prohibited in 1974.[84] In this way of receiving communion, it is less clear that we "receive" the eucharistic gift; it is also less hygienic.

Receiving communion in processional form and singing together can manifest its ecclesial dimension, especially when we make a half circle around the altar, the table of the Lord. When this is feasible, it is more expressive than when the priest or minister remains in one spot.

About communion from the chalice, the General Instruction, in article 245, provides for four forms:

> The Blood of the Lord may be consumed either by drinking from the chalice directly, or by intinction, or by means of a tube or a spoon.

Drinking from the chalice seems to be the most expressive form of receiving the Blood, corresponding to the sign instituted by Christ. Recourse to a drinking straw is a rather cumbersome, embarrassing,

83. *Notitiae* 5 (1969) 353.
84. *Notitiae* 10 (1974) 308.

and unattractive act. Nevertheless, we find in the Roman ordines the use of a *pugillaris, calamus,* or *fistula* as this was called.[85] The use of a small spoon to place the contents of the chalice on the tongue of the communicant seems, for Western people, rather puerile, although it is usual in the Byzantine rite. This method also retains communion on the tongue. Distribution of the Precious Blood by a spoon or through a straw is not customary in the Latin dioceses of the United States of America.[86]

The General Instruction gives the following description of communion from the chalice and communion by intinction:

> If Communion of the Blood of Christ is carried out by communicants' drinking from the chalice, each communicant, after receiving the Body of Christ, moves to the minister of the chalice and stands facing him. The minister says, The Blood of Christ, the communicant replies, Amen, and the minister hands over the chalice, which the communicant raises to his or her mouth. Each communicant drinks a little from the chalice, hands it back to the minister, and then withdraws; the minister wipes the rim of the chalice with the purificator. (GIRM 286)

> If Communion from the chalice is carried out by intinction, each communicant, holding a Communion-plate under the mouth, approaches the Priest who holds a vessel with the sacred particles, with a minister standing at his side and holding the chalice. The Priest takes a host, intincts it partly in the chalice and, showing it, says, The Body and Blood of Christ. The communicant replies, Amen, receives the Sacrament in the mouth from the Priest, and then withdraws. (GIRM 287)

Regarding communion from the chalice by intinction, the Norms for the Distribution and Reception of Holy Communion Under Both Kinds in the Dioceses of the United States of America stipulates:

> 49. Holy Communion may be distributed by intinction in the following manner: Each communicant, while holding a Communion-

---

85. E.g., " . . . et tradit calicem subdiacono regionario, qui tradit ei pugillarem cum quo confirmat populum." *Ordo Romanus I,* n. 20.

86. Norms for the Distribution and Reception of Holy Communion Under Both Kinds in the Dioceses of the United States of America, art. 48.

plate under the mouth, approaches the Priest who holds a vessel with the sacred particles, with a minister standing at his side and holding the chalice. The Priest takes a host, intincts it partly in the chalice and, showing it, says: "The Body and Blood of Christ." The communicant replies, "Amen," receives the Sacrament in the mouth from the Priest, and then withdraws.

50. The communicant, including the extraordinary minister, is never allowed to self-communicate, even by means of intinction. Communion under either form, bread or wine, must always be given by an ordinary or extraordinary minister of Holy Communion.

This way of intinction, however, retains communion on the tongue and makes receiving the bread in the hand impossible. Therefore, we can raise the question of self-intinction, as practiced in some regions. Here the communicant receives the host in his or her hand that is given by one minister, then steps to the side to dip the host partly in the chalice that is presented by another minister. The communicant holds her or his hand under the dipped host to avoid drops and brings it into her or his mouth.

This way of receiving both kinds preserves the truth present in the more complete sign. It is also a more mature way. There is not at all a danger for profanation of the Eucharist as some may pretend. It can also express the necessary attitude of humble receptivity because in this way we do not directly "take" the sacrament but "receive" it. In addition, when we receive the chalice from a minister we take it in our hands and drink from it. The minister does not bring the chalice to our mouth! By self-intinction we first receive the host in the palm of our hand before we dip it in the chalice. Some see the fact that the traitor Judas dipped his bread in the dish as a reason against self-intinction, but we forget that the other apostles probably did as well. Therefore, this seems a rather ridiculous argument against self-intinction.

Indeed, in its instruction *Redemptionis Sacramentum* of March 25, 2004, the Congregation for Divine Worship and the Discipline of the Sacraments still stipulated:

> As regards the administering of Communion to lay members of Christ's faithful, the Bishops may exclude Communion with the

tube or the spoon where this is not the local custom, though the option of administering Communion by intinction always remains. If this modality is employed, however, hosts should be used which are neither too thin nor too small, and the communicant should receive the Sacrament from the Priest only on the tongue. The communicant must not be permitted to intinct the host himself in the chalice, nor to receive the intincted host in the hand. As for the host to be used for the intinction, it should be made of valid matter, also consecrated; it is altogether forbidden to use non-consecrated bread or other matter.[87]

The Communion Chant. The General Instruction describes the role of the communion chant as follows:

> While the priest is receiving the Sacrament, the Communion chant is begun, its purpose being to express the spiritual union of the communicants by means of the unity of their voices, to show gladness of heart, and to bring out more clearly the "communitarian" character of the procession to receive the Eucharist. The singing is prolonged for as long as the Sacrament is being administered to the faithful. However, if there is to be a hymn after Communion, the Communion Chant should be ended in a timely manner.
>
> Care should be taken that singers, too, can receive Communion with ease. (GIRM 86)

Where the Latin text of article 87 speaks about *alius cantus congruus a Conferentia Episcoporum approbatus*, the approved English text for the United States interpreted this article as follows:

> In the Dioceses of the United States of America, there are four options for singing at Communion: (1) the antiphon from the Missal or the antiphon with its Psalm from the Graduale Romanum, as set to music there or in another musical setting; (2) the antiphon with Psalm from the Graduale Simplex of the liturgical time; (3) a chant from another collection of Psalms and antiphons, approved by the Conference of Bishops or the Diocesan Bishop, including Psalms arranged in responsorial or metrical forms; (4) some other suitable

---

87. *Redemptionis Sacramentum.* On certain matters to be observed or to be avoided regarding the Most Holy Eucharist, art. 103–104.

liturgical chant (cf. no. 86) approved by the Conference of Bishops or the Diocesan Bishop. This is sung either by the choir alone or by the choir or a cantor with the people.

However, if there is no singing, the antiphon given in the Missal may be recited either by the faithful, or by some of them, or by a reader; otherwise, it is recited by the Priest himself after he has received Communion and before he distributes Communion to the faithful. (GIRM 87)

In its view of the meaning and function of the communion chant, the General Instruction is in line with the original function of this element. In the fourth century, the chant already existed as a responsorial song, in which the cantor sang the psalm verses and the people always replied with the same repeated verse. It was a chant accompanying the procession of the faithful to the altar and back to their places. Cyril of Jerusalem testifies:

> After this you hear the chanter inviting you with a divine melody to the partaking of the holy mysteries, in the words "Taste and see that the Lord is good."[88]

The communicants originally participated in the communion song, but in later times the *schola cantorum* seems to have taken over all or part of this song, because the melodies were enriched and the texts expanded. Even in the Roman liturgy, they initially stuck to singing the psalm. The papal liturgy, as described in the *Ordo Romanus I*, teaches us that the *schola cantorum* started with the communion antiphon when the pope began the distribution of communion. Then the psalmody followed and when communion ended, the archdeacon gave a sign on which the *Gloria Patri* was sung and the antiphon was repeated. In short, the same method was used here as with the entrance song. The communion song therefore functioned as an accompanying song at communion.

From the thirteenth century onwards only the antiphon was preserved, which was called *communio*. When in this period the

---

88. Cyrillus Hieros., "Catecheses Mystagogicae Quinque, V 20," *PG* 33, k. 1123. English translation Sheerin, *o.c.*, 72.

communion of the faithful had almost completely decayed, the communion song lost its meaning and ended up after the communion of the priest, even after the ablutions. The *communio* was more and more regarded as a prayer of thanks, which is actually the meaning of the *postcommunio*. Thus, the *communio* ended up in the Missal of Trent, where it completely lost its meaning as accompanying song for the communion of the faith community.

The instruction *De musica sacra et sacra liturgia* of September 3, 1958, restored the *communio* as chant during the communion.[89] The General Instruction continues this improvement and makes the communion chant again the accompanying song during the communion rite of the whole community of faith. It is sung as soon as the priest receives communion and continues normally until all have received communion.

It is important that everyone actually participates in this song because of its community-building character. As the entrance song expresses that we have come together as a unanimous community to celebrate the Eucharist, the communion song expresses that, through communion, we not only become one with Christ but, precisely because of that, become one with each other. By eating the Eucharist, the Body of Christ, we all become together the ecclesial Body of Christ.

Communicating together while singing also confirms the combination of word and sacrament. When God's word, the promised salvation, is sacramentally realized to us through communion, we sing about this word. If possible, it would therefore be desirable for a particular aspect of the Liturgy of the Word to be found in the communion chant.

Some Conclusions Related to Active Participation

When we look at the whole of the communion rite, the following can be said in connection with active participation. First of all, in the renewed rite the communion of the faithful is no longer detached from the communion of the priest. Further, it is no longer regarded as a possibility but as an integral part of the celebration. It is certainly encouraging to see how the faithful now experience this as self-evident.

---

89. "Instructio 'De musica sacra et sacra liturgia,'" *AAS* 50 (1958) 630–663, n. 27, p. 640–641.

By allowing the faithful to receive communion as much as possible with hosts that are consecrated in the Mass in which they participate, their communion is experienced as a real participation in the celebration itself. Nevertheless, we see that in some parishes priests continue to use hosts mainly from the tabernacle, not to supplement a possible shortage of freshly consecrated and broken hosts, but rather in principle. Have they not yet understood, after fifty years of liturgical renewal, how wrong the image of the eucharistic celebration is that they present? Do they not realize the injustice they do to the celebrating community over which they preside? Even though the communion of the faithful immediately connects with that of the priest, the use of pre-consecrated hosts from the Holy Reserve makes it a stand-alone event.

This experience of a stand-alone event is also influenced by the fact that in some parishes, there cannot be a eucharistic celebration every Sunday because of the shortage of priests. In this case, there is a so-called Sunday Celebration in the Absence of a Priest, mainly a Liturgy of Word and Prayer. But completely against the meaning of such a celebration, here too communion is usually distributed,[90] of course, with pre-consecrated hosts.[91] It is therefore understandable that many faithful do not see the difference with a eucharistic celebration, where a ciborium with pre-consecrated hosts is also taken from the tabernacle. As we have seen, in some parishes the lay-"presider" stands behind the altar all the time: confusion complete![92]

We can honestly say that this is not a eucharistic celebration, but for people's lived experience it is very similar, so people are satisfied.

90. Note that the Directory does not say that communion must be distributed: "The faithful are to understand that the Eucharistic sacrifice cannot take place without a priest and that the Eucharistic *communion which they may receive* in this kind of assembly is closely connected with the sacrifice of the Mass" (art. 23).

91. Indeed, the Directory for Sunday Celebrations in the Absence of a Priest (June 2, 1988) foresees such distribution of communion—this in a time when we have rediscovered and restored the union between communion and eucharistic celebration. As long as one sees the illogic of distributing pre-consecrated hosts during a eucharistic celebration, one shall not make big problems by giving communion outside the eucharistic celebration.

92. They have transformed the "table of the Lord" into a desk.

We already hear people speaking about a lay Mass, a sister's Mass. From a pastoral point of view some think that when no communion is given, the number of participants decreases.[93] In every way, we have to express that the communion service is never to be seen as an independent celebration. It must always be brought into connection with an earlier eucharistic celebration or with the celebration of the Eucharist in another place nearby. The latter is a better way to express the unity of our celebration with the Eucharist, especially when the eucharistic bread is brought from a church nearby where at the same moment Christians are effectively celebrating the Eucharist.

Communion services show our lack of faith in Christ' presence in his church. There is a certain gradation in the way he is present. Have we forgotten or do we neglect what Vatican II said in the Constitution on the Sacred Liturgy?

> Christ is always present in his church, especially in liturgical cele-brations. He is present in the sacrifice of the Mass . . . and most of all in the eucharistic species. By his power he is present in the sacraments. . . . He is present in his word, since it is he himself who speaks when the holy scriptures are read in church. Lastly, he is present when the church prays and sings, for he has promised "where two or three are gathered together in my name there am I in the midst of them" (Mt 18:20). (SC 7)

This means that when we gather as a community on the Lord's Day and we cannot celebrate the Eucharist we must be aware that Christ is already present in the fact that we are assembled in his name. His presence is more expressive when we receive him through his word, which we celebrate in joy and gratitude, and when we meet him in our prayer and singing. When there is no priest among us, we cannot go further to celebrate the Eucharist and consequently, we should not meet Christ through communion. In a certain sense, then, we do not have a Sunday Celebration in the Absence of a Priest, but a Sunday Celebration in the Expectation of a Priest. In France, for instance, they speak not only about *Assemblée Domini-*

93. In our days, when within the ecumenical movement there is a great agree-ment about the theology and the practice of the Lord's Supper, our growing practice of communion services is astonishing for our brothers and sisters from the Reformation.

cale en l'Absence du Prêtre, but also about *Assemblée Dominicale en l'Attente du Prêtre*.

Through this formulation, we express that this kind of Sunday celebration is not the normal situation, that sometimes we live in a situation of emergency, and that we hope that soon a priest may preside over our eucharistic celebration on Sunday. Therefore, we have to pray for and to promote vocations, knowing that "the stork [does not] bring priests."[94] And we have to pray that the church authorities may change the conditions for ordination, so that married men and women can become priests. Why not? In the meantime—but let us hope that it is not too long a time—we shall celebrate Sunday as a community of Christians in the absence and in the expectation of a priest. As faithful, we have to claim our right to a Sunday eucharistic celebration. The church authorities must not escape their responsibility by offering us an easy, pseudo-solution in the form of a communion service.

Continuing with our conclusions, we can say that what is also important for active participation is the answer to the invitation to receive communion as a common act of humility, of an awareness of unworthiness.

The accompanying formula for communion requires the communicant to express an active confession of faith and the willingness for Christian engagement. Active participation here is clearly much more than being allowed to say or do something but involves the whole personality in the celebration.

Since the norm now for the reception of communion is standing, we can experience this as an active expression of reverence, and of the fact that as baptized people we participate in Christ's paschal mystery. It can surely be helpful to provide the faithful with proper catechesis on the reasons for this norm.

The personal acceptance of the host in the palm of the hand can also be an expression of conscious acceptance of the eucharistic bread given to us by the Lord as a sign of his total self-giving for our salvation.

The introduction of communion under both kinds principally removes the distinction between priest and lay faithful regarding the full sign of communion. It can therefore be an important element

94. M. Sheehan, "Sunday Worship Without a Priest," *Origins* 21 (1992) 621–625, 621.

to participate more intensely and actively in the eucharistic celebration. The most appropriate here is without a doubt communion by drinking from the chalice. While there is only one large chalice on the altar during the eucharistic prayer, just as there is also only one large paten with hosts, the content of this large chalice can be distributed among several small chalices just before communion. In this way the faithful can explicitly receive the eucharistic bread and wine. Communion by intinction according to the prescribed procedure has the great disadvantage that, once again, the priest puts the host and the wine directly into the mouth of the faithful. Here we want to clearly argue for the official admission of communion by self-intinction.

In the United States, we can conclude that slightly less than half the parishes offer the assembly access to the cup. We must notice that in different parts of the Western world a great number of parishes rarely or never provide the possibility to receive communion under both kinds for the faithful. Even worse is that most of those faithful do not seem to mind this! Is this the result of a lack of liturgical catechesis? How does this impact our ideal of active participation?

The communion chant as accompanying song can also be an important element of active participation because it expresses the communal character of receiving communion as unification with Christ and with each other. We thereby sing our belief that in the communion rite God's offer of salvation, proclaimed in the Liturgy of the Word, is realized sacramentally to us.

One negative in the renewed communion rite may be seen in the personal preparatory prayer of the priest and the formulas at his communion. This still preserves the former distinction between priest and laity at the very moment when we celebrate our unity sacramentally with God and with each other.

Purification, the Prayer in Silence, and the Prayer after Communion

The Purification

It is remarkable that article 88 of the General Instruction does not speak about the purification of the sacred vessels, but immediately states that "the priest and faithful spend some time praying privately." In its description of the Mass with a Congregation, however, we find the following:

When the distribution of Communion is over . . . Upon returning to the altar, the Priest collects the fragments, should any remain, and he stands at the altar or at the credence table and purifies the paten or ciborium over the chalice, and after this purifies the chalice, saying quietly the formula Quod ore sumpsimus, Domine (What has passed our lips), and dries the chalice with a purificator. If the vessels are purified at the altar, they are carried to the credence table by a minister. Nevertheless, it is also permitted to leave vessels needing to be purified, especially if there are several, on a corporal, suitably covered, either on the altar or on the credence table, and to purify them immediately after Mass, after the Dismissal of the people. (GIRM 163)

This rite is simplified when we compare it with the former rite. From a prior, fearful attitude that no miniscule part of the host or a drop of the sacred Blood may be lost, we came to a mature attitude of respect for the consecrated gifts. The Lord is present among us under the appearances of bread and wine that are recognizable as such. There is no reason to search with microscopic accuracy for possible particles. This does not mean that we can be negligent in dealing with the sacred gifts.[95]

In fact, the purification is not part of the essential elements of the eucharistic celebration, so that, as the General Instruction also allows, one can immediately bring dish and cup to the credence table and do the purification after the celebration.[96] In this case the prayer "Lord, may I receive" falls away. After all, this prayer is by origin not an ablution prayer but a *postcommunio*.

95. The difficulties arise from an exaggerated application of the doctrine of transubstantiation. This doctrine means that the substance of the Body of Christ is present in the place of the substance of the bread, without changing the appearance of the bread. When the consecrated bread is broken, the Body of Christ is not broken: every part of the broken bread presents the Body of Christ. Hence, the fear that very small particles would be lost. This was also expressed in the former liturgy of the Mass in the fact that from the consecration to the cleansing of the chalice the priest had to keep the tips of the index finger and thumb together and cleanse these fingers. Today we argue that there can only be the presence of Christ's Body as long as the appearance of bread is present to the natural senses.

96. In daily life, we do not wash the dishes and the cutlery at the table!

The Silent Prayer

In the description of the Mass with a Congregation we find:

> After this, the Priest may return to the chair. A sacred silence may now be observed for some time, or a Psalm or other canticle of praise or a hymn may be sung (cf. no. 88). (GIRM 164)

This article speaks about a "sacred silence." The Council expressly asked that such moments in the eucharistic celebration be provided (SC 30). If a moment of silence is desirable anywhere in the liturgy it is here, so that everyone can reflect on the mystery of communion in gratitude. Personal prayer here does not mean private prayer, so it is better to speak of a common silent prayer, a prayer in silence that happens in communion. This common silent prayer is also a liturgical act and is recognized as such by the General Instruction. The personal prayer of all is indeed "collected" when the priest prays the final prayer in his function as presider.

Such moments of common silence are rare in the liturgy. We want to fill everything up with prayers, readings, and chants. Have we really understood what active participation is if we let the faithful say and do as much as possible in the liturgy, but not ensure their prayer and faith life is deepened and nourished? Should there not be room for personal integration and confirmation of what we have done, sang, and prayed together? We ask the faithful to answer "Amen" when the priest offers them the Body (and Blood) of Christ, but are they given the opportunity to personally integrate, in a moment of silent prayer, this testimony of faith and willingness for Christian engagement? Is our liturgy, especially here, at the summit of active participation that communion should be, not threatened by formalism? Do we think too easily that we have reached our goal when the faithful answer, sing, and approach the holy table? Active participation is first and foremost an entry into the paschal mystery of Christ that is present within the community of faith. To pray together, sing together, and act together, but also to be silent together, are ultimately what make this participation in Christ's paschal mystery possible and enable us to express it.

The importance of this silent prayer after communion has become even greater because the custom of remaining in the church for a short period of time after the celebration in personal thanksgiving has almost disappeared.[97] The integration of this silent prayer within the community is a significant improvement. Of course, this practice must not create the impression of an arbitrary lengthening of the Mass.

Article 164 of the General Instruction provides for the priest to return to his chair after communion and sit down with the faithful. It seems appropriate that the purification is not done at this time, but that the altar server or minister brings the cup and paten to the credence table. It is worthwhile here for the priest to introduce the common silent prayer by the invitation, "Let us pray."

Article 164 also provides the possibility of singing "a Psalm or another canticle of praise or a hymn . . . " Yet singing seems less desirable here for two reasons. First, this important moment of silent prayer is then lost. Second, it seems an unnecessary doubling of the communion song, although the communion chant is an accompanying song and this song would have the character of praise and thanksgiving. We can also use such a song when the priest leaves the altar.

The Prayer after Communion

Then, standing at the chair or at the altar, and facing the people with hands joined, the Priest says, Let us pray; then, with hands extended, he recites the Prayer after Communion. A brief period of silence may precede the prayer, unless this has been already observed immediately after Communion. At the end of the prayer the people acclaim, Amen. (GIRM 165)

As the collect is the recapitulation and conclusion of the introductory rite, the prayer of the faithful the conclusion of the Liturgy of the Word, and the prayer over the gifts the ending of the preparation of the gifts, the prayer after communion concludes the Liturgy of the Eucharist. In this prayer, the priest not only collects the personal, silent prayer of the community, but also summarizes and concludes the entire Liturgy of the Eucharist in which we, after sacramentally making present Christ's paschal mystery through praise, thanksgiving,

---

97. Indeed, after the dismissal the people take literally what is told to them, namely, to depart.

anamnesis, epiclesis, and offering, participated through communion. Since the prayer after communion frequently refers to the essential ideas of the Liturgy of the Word, we can also consider it as the conclusion of the entire celebration.

Saying the prayer from either the chair or the altar can be defended. When one considers the prayer as the conclusion of the Liturgy of the Eucharist, the altar seems to be the right place for it. When one wants to consider it from a broader perspective, as the conclusion of both the Liturgy of the Word and the Liturgy of the Eucharist, the chair seems a better fit. Indeed, when the celebrant goes to his chair for the common silent prayer it seems obvious that the prayer after communion be said there, and then the priest returns to the altar for the concluding rites.

As the silent prayer is introduced by "Let us pray," it is evident that the priest does not need to say this again. The prayer after communion is a presidential prayer that presupposes, of course, the acclamation of the faith community on behalf of whom the prayer is said. The "Amen" at this moment is therefore an important element of active participation.

This becomes even clearer when we analyze the content of the prayer. There is always an allusion to the sacred meal in which we have participated, both personally and as a community. It states in some way what this brings about for us: grace, sanctification, healing, purification, strength, unity, mutual love, and so on. It says, in effect, "Thanks for all of this." This thanksgiving immediately leads to a supplication for the future, and even to the ultimate future: that we may live every day from the unity that we were allowed to celebrate in the meal as a pledge of eternal life. In its conciseness, the prayer after communion always has a thankful, petitioning, personal, ecclesial, and eschatological character. When we bring all this together, we would dare to call the prayer after communion a theology of the Eucharist in the shape of prayer.

Chapter Four

The Concluding Rites

The concluding rites can consist of brief announcements and concluding comments, greeting the congregation, a blessing and dismissal, veneration of the altar, and the recessional.

Announcements and Concluding Comment

Announcements

Where formerly the announcements came before the homily, the General Instruction designates the concluding rites as the most appropriate moment so that they least disturb the course of the liturgical event. The announcements must be limited to the most essential ones, and only be given if needed. There are other means for extensive announcements, for example, the church website and the parish bulletin.

Concluding Comments

The concluding comments are of a completely different nature. They allow the presider to recall briefly the main idea of the Liturgy of the Word or the specific aspect of the celebration in short and more personal words. He might also try to make a connection with the everyday life to which the faithful now return. Thus, the link between liturgy and life is made clear to the faithful. In this sense, active participation in the eucharistic celebration is extended to an active commitment to daily life. In this way the liturgy really becomes the source of true Christian life. Most important, we must avoid making these concluding words a second homily, nor can we reduce them to a wish for a pleasant Sunday.

Blessing and Dismissal

Greeting of the Congregation

Before the blessing we have the last of the four greetings that the renewed liturgy has retained. The three other greetings are found at the introductory rites, the gospel reading, and the preface.

Blessing

The blessing by the priest at the end of the eucharistic celebration has not existed for too long. Originally, only the bishop gave the blessing after the Mass, when he had left the altar, and only when the faithful had asked for it. Later, on Frankish soil, priests also claimed the right to give the blessing after the Mass. Until the twelfth century, the liturgical books do not mention a blessing by the priest from the altar. Afterwards, when the blessing was generally given from the altar, it happened after the *ite, missa est.* The Tridentine Missal then confirmed this procedure, in such a way that until 1969,[1] the blessing was given after the dismissal. Fortunately, the faithful waited for the blessing.

The new Missal reversed the sequence logically. Now the priest blesses the people with the formula, "May Almighty God bless you, the Father, and the Son, and the Holy Spirit," and all answer "Amen" (GIRM 167).

Solemn Blessing and Prayer over the People

In article 167, the General Instruction also provides that

> [o]n certain days and occasions this blessing, in accordance with the rubrics, is expanded and expressed by a Prayer over the People or another more solemn formula.

The Roman Missal has a section following immediately after the order of Mass containing twenty solemn blessings and twenty-eight prayers over the people for specific times and seasons of the year.[2]

---

1. The "missa normative," as presented to the 1967 Synod of Bishops, already had the sequence greeting, blessing, and dismissal.

2. Msgr. Walter Dürig of the University of Munich and consultor of the Consilium proposed in 1969 to reintroduce these solemn blessings. Walter Dürig, "Der Entlassungssegen in der Messfeier. Anregungen zu einer Reform," *Liturgisches Jahrbuch* 19 (1969) 205–218.

The solemn blessings are inspired by the Gallican *Benedictiones epico-pales* and consist of three strophes to which the faithful always reply "Amen."[3] The blessing by the priest follows after the last "Amen." These expansions offer the possibility to enrich the blessing with appropriate aspects and to interpret them.

The prayer over the people formed the end of the eucharistic liturgy in the oldest liturgy. Also, the previous Missal kept a remnant of such prayers on ferial days in Lent, introduced by "Bow your heads for God." The 1970 Missal revived them. Some people, however, experience them as a second prayer after communion and as such, repetitious.

Dismissal

The revised Missal provided one single formula for the dismissal. In the Latin text it is, *Ite, missa est*, and the people answer, *Deo gratias* (GIRM 168). This means that the *Benedicamus Domino* in Masses without the Gloria and *Requiescant in pace* in Masses for the dead have been eliminated. In most languages, *Ite missa est* is currently translated as "The Mass is ended, go in peace." The people's answer in the formula is translated as, "Thanks be to God."

In 2008 Pope Benedict XVI, along with the official translation, "Go forth, the Mass is ended," allowed the use of three other formulas.[4] The ICEL text provides as translations, "Go in the peace of Christ," "The Mass is ended, go in peace," or "Go in peace to love and serve the Lord." These formulas are the result of an idea raised at the 2005 Synod of Bishops on the Eucharist. Many bishops wanted the formula to reflect a more explicit connection between Mass and our mission of evangelization in the world.

The formula "go in peace" is not a subtlety. It is derived from the Eastern liturgies because the Latin formula was mostly misinterpreted

---

3. E.g., "In Adventu: Omnípotens et miséricors Deus, cuius Unigéniti advéntum et praetéritum créditis, et futúrum exspectátis, eiúsdem advéntus vos illustratióne sanctíficet et sua benedictióne locuplétet. R/. Amen. In praeséntis vitae stádio reddat vos in fide stabiles spe gaudéntes, et in caritáte efficáces. R/. Amen. Ut, qui de advéntu Redemptóris nostri secúndum carnem devóta mente laetámini, in secúndo, cum in maiestáte sua vénerit, praemiis aetérnae vitae ditémini. R/. Amen. Et benedíctio Dei omnipoténtis, Patris, et Filii, ✠ et Spíritus Sancti, descéndat super vos et máneat semper. R/. Amen."

4. In Latin: *"Ite ad Evangelium Domini annuntiandum," "Ite in pace, glorificando vita vestra Dominum," "Ite in pace."*

and misunderstood. The Latin *missa* originally had the meaning of *mission*, or dismissal. This formula was used in ancient Rome for the dissolution of a meeting. *Ite, missa est* can be translated then as "Go, this is the dismissal" or "Go, the meeting is concluded." Gradually, from the fourth century onward, the church began to see *missa* more in the sense of *oblatio* and it became the denomination of the entire eucharistic celebration. The formula *ite, missa est* up to our time was translated as "Go forth, the Mass is ended." Gradually we once again began to link the word *missa* with "mission." That idea played a role in Pope Benedict XVI's decision to allow the alternate translations.[5]

In the 1970 Missal, *ite, missa est* returned to its function as a dismissal formula. Logically, it is omitted if another liturgical action follows immediately and the people are therefore not dismissed.

Our formula "go in peace," as we have already said, is derived from the Eastern liturgies, where they did not choose the business-like dismissal of a meeting, as in the Latin expression, but instead gave the dismissal a biblical dimension. With that, they referred to Luke 7:50, where Jesus says to the penitent sinful woman, "Your faith has saved you; go in peace" (cf. Mark 5:34). This is what we still find in the Byzantine rite: *en eirènè proelthoomen* ("Let us go in peace"). In the West, more precisely in the Ambrosian liturgy, they used the formula *procedamus in pace* and *in nomine Domini* as the answer of the people.

Kissing the Altar, Reverence, and Departure

After the blessing and the dismissal, the priest greets the altar with a kiss and a gesture of reverence, as he did at the beginning. The priest gives the kiss in silence, because this gesture is expressive as such. The gesture of reverence consists ordinarily in making a profound bow.

Then the priest and his ministers leave the altar while the people leave the church. In some parishes, a meaningful custom exists to remain together for a while on the church grounds or in the parish house. In this way, they solidify the link between the eucharistic celebration and daily Christian life.

---

5. Pope Benedict XVI, post-synodal apostolic exhortation *Sacramentum Caritatis* (Vatican City, 2007), n. 51.

The whole of the Concluding Rites appears to be clear in its conciseness, which benefits active participation. After all, the faithful are very clearly involved in these concluding rites.

Epilogue

In the first part of this book, we showed how the 1970 Missal in its guiding principles is in line with the desire of the Second Vatican Council to make active participation of the lay faithful an integral element of the renewed eucharistic celebration. In the second part, we examined to what extent the set principles were taken into account in the various parts and rites of the eucharistic celebration. We can call the result of this research quite positive, although in a number of places, either due to a lack of clarity, because of overload, or because of a remnant of clerical distinction, we had to point out a hindrance to true communal celebration. In certain places, we encountered the regrettable consequences of compromises that apparently were made within the Consilium. Here and there we also formulated a number of desires and proposals that, according to our opinion, can contribute to a truly ecclesial liturgy.

Whether or not we obtain the desired communal celebration with the active participation of all does not depend solely on the Missal. The faith community of priest and laity must realize the possibilities offered by a true ecclesial liturgy. Fifty years after the publication of the revised Roman Missal, it is and remains primarily a matter of liturgical pastoral care and catechesis. In our study of the Missal, we constantly pointed out the importance of this. Indeed, according to article 34 of the Constitution on the Sacred Liturgy the rites should be distinguished by a "noble simplicity," should be within the people's power of comprehension, and normally should not require much explanation. This was not always taken fully into account in the renewed Missal. Even if all rites were equally clear, however, liturgical pastoral care and catechesis would be necessary. After all, liturgical formation is more than gaining insight into the meaning and coherence of the different liturgical rites. Liturgical formation is mainly connected with learning to live in the spirit of

liturgy, with an awareness of one's own task in the liturgical meetings of the local ecclesia.

It is therefore not sufficient to celebrate the Eucharist according to the new regulations, to appoint some readers, to learn new
church songs, to ask the faithful to give certain answers, and so on.
All this only makes sense when, at the same time, the faithful learn to
discover what the celebration of the Eucharist actually means. Only
when the grounding experience of what unites them as ecclesia to
celebrate the Eucharist is evoked in a perceptible way, a community
can come to repeat with full devotion the liturgical ritual as manifestation, perception, intensification, and regeneration of its identity.

In our catechesis, therefore, we must work on helping the faithful experience themselves, through their baptism and confirmation,
as people of God who come together in the Eucharist around the
celebration of the mysteries of faith. In this way they can give to the
Father, in the unity of the Spirit with and through Christ, the perfect
thanks and honor. Liturgical pastoral care should concern itself with
taking care of the liturgical meetings in order to make these, with
the possibilities and room for creativity provided by the Missal, into
real celebrations around the Lord who is present among us in his
Word and Sacrament.